ENDORSEM

"Chris Humphrey embodies true worship from every very fiber and core of his being unlike anyone I personally know! He is a passionate pursuer of the Presence of God during mundane times of driving down the highway in his car all the way to the twenty- four to fifty-hour Burn events he hosts every month in Northern California! Many times he does not leave the room for the entire period! I cannot think of a better heart and life to model and articulate the values, principles, and testimonies from a life lived in the perpetual place of worship!"

—Sean Feucht
Founder of Burn 24-7

"Chris is one of the most humble, authentic, and passionate men that I know. His life and testimony are a beautiful picture of the radical and transforming love of God. Chris is a true father to a broken generation and has an incredible anointing to raise up spiritual sons and daughters. His life message will inspire and challenge you to fall deeper in love with Jesus and to be a whole-hearted, sacrificial servant of the gospel."

—David Fritch
Burn 24-7

"Chris Humphrey has a heart of David! One that has the courage to serve the purpose of God in his generation, marked by the raw reality of God. And, in his journey, he offers fresh language to the hungry pilgrim."

—Roger Joyner
Prayer Leader

"Chris Humphrey has been a father to my life, a man of prayer and faithfulness to the call of God. I believe these pages you read will truly impart that. The years sown in tears will see its fruit in this generation."

—BRIAN BARCELONA
One Voice Student Missions

"Chris Humphrey is the definition of what a whole-hearted radical lover of God is! He has a contagious passion that draws people into the glorious Presence of The Lord. When you read this book you will experience the love that has made Chris a reckless abandoned worshiper of God!"

—JARROD MCEACHRON
Student Ministries Director
Harvest Church, Elk Grove CA

For the last few years I've had the joy of knowing Chris and watching God move through his life. He is a man on fire; a fire that is mingled with humility and integrity. That fire and passion will be imparted as you journey through the chapters of this book.

—CALEB KLINGE
Senior Pastor
New Life Christian Center, Novato CA

This book paints a picture of the true heart of God and His never-ending love for us. We are created for God's pleasure! Chris Humphrey's life is proof that God takes joy in each of us as we take joy in abiding in His love and live a life of worship."

—STEPHEN STOCKLIN
Burn 24-7 Seattle/Port Orchard

THE END TIME WORSHIP ARMY

CHOOSING A LIFE OF WORSHIP THAT CHANGES CITIES AND NATIONS

CHRIS HUMPHREY

© 2014 by Chris Humphrey

Paperback ISBN-13: 978-1499377859
E-book ISBN-13: 978-1483528007

Published by
Chris and Alycia Humphrey
Burn 24-7 Sacramento
Contact the author at chrish@theburn247.com

No part of this book may be reproduced, stored in a retrieval system or transmitted in any form or by any means – electronic, mechanical, photocopy, recording or any other – except for brief quotations, without permission in writing from the publisher.

Scripture taken from THE HOLY BIBLE, NEW INTERNATIONAL VERSION®, NIV® Copyright © 1973, 1978, 1984, 2011 by Biblica, Inc.® Used by permission. All rights reserved worldwide.

Scripture quotations marked (NKJV) are taken from the New King James Version®. Copyright © 1982 by Thomas Nelson, Inc. Used by permission. All rights reserved.

Scripture quotations marked (NLT) are taken from the Holy Bible, New Living Translation, copyright © 1996, 2004, 2007 by Tyndale House Foundation. Used by permission of Tyndale House Publishers, Inc., Carol Stream, Illinois 60188. All rights reserved.

Scripture quotations marked NASB are taken from the NEW AMERICAN STANDARD BIBLE®, Copyright © 1960, 1962, 1963, 1968, 1971, 1972, 1973, 1975, 1977, 1995 by The Lockman Foundation. Used by permission.

Cover design by Yvonne Parks at www.pearcreative.ca
Interior design and typesetting by Katherine Lloyd at www.theDESKonline.com

CONTENTS

Introduction 9

PART ONE: TRUE WORSHIP

Chapter 1: THE HEART OF WORSHIP 15

Chapter 2: WHO DO YOU WORSHIP? 31

Chapter 3: THE OBJECT OF OUR AFFECTION 43

Chapter 4: WORSHIP IN THE WILDERNESS 59

Chapter 5: SWEET SMELLING FRAGRANCE 77

Chapter 6: THE FRUIT OF WORSHIP 93

Chapter 7: ABIDING IN THE VINE 107

PART TWO: THE END TIME ARMY

Chapter 8: THE DAVIDIC GENERATION 125

Chapter 9: LEGACY FOR ALL GENERATIONS 139

Chapter 10: THE BURNING ONES 157

Chapter 11: THE BELOVED BRIDE 169

Chapter 12: WARRING FROM HIS PRESENCE 181

ACKNOWLEDGEMENTS

I truly want to give special thanks to my wife, Alycia. She is the greatest gift from God that I have received in this life. Thank you, my love, for standing by me through every trial. Thank you for encouraging me through this journey. I am so thankful that you said yes to marrying a man who was fresh out of prison. You saw in me what I never imagined in myself. You took a risk marrying me and your risk has helped me to become a better man! I love you so much.

My mom and dad, James and Felicia! You have made this book possible through being an amazing family who has seen me go through the crazy things and you never gave up on me. Thank you for believing in me. Mom, thank you for always demonstrating unconditional love. Dad, thank you for your example of an honest, hard-working man. James and Felicia, thank you for investing into my life.

I would also like to thank Sean Feucht and my entire Burn 24-7 family. Sean, your crazy, radical life has inspired me to greatness. My Burn family, you always impart hope to me as I hear all the radical stories of what God is doing in your cities worldwide through your simple yes to Burn night and day.

Nancy King and Justina Harston. Your work and awesome editing skills took this project beyond what I was capable. Your hard work has not gone unnoticed. You are both greatly appreciated.

Last of all, and more the inspiration behind it all, Jesus! He is my beautiful Lord. His gracious gift of His Abiding Presence has inspired every one of us to live a life full of His goodness. Thank you so much, Lord Jesus. It is worth every bit of whatever we have to walk through in this life to catch just one glimpse of Your Eternal Glory. I love you so much, Lord.

Introduction

MY STORY

You are about to embark on a journey, but before you go any further, I want to share my story with you. Perhaps an inside look into what I have walked through as a worshiper of God will help you grasp what God is saying to you. Within these pages you will read both deep scriptural revelation regarding the life of worship and personal experiences and examples that I believe will help you on your journey. My prayer is that, as you read through this book, God will take you into the same places He took me as I wrote my heart for all to see.

My story is quite different than what you might think. Unlike many of my contemporaries, I was neither raised in revival nor mentored by a great father in the church. In fact, I wasn't even raised in the house of God. The truth is that my past is riddled with excessive drug use and experimentation with witchcraft and New Age spirits. My experiences took me down a path of extreme darkness that only Jesus could deliver me from. Some of my closest friends during this period of my life are now either dead or serving life in prison. My testimony does not include being born into the great revival that is currently being poured out on the church. Nonetheless, every testimony carries within it the prophetic DNA to reveal Jesus Christ. Mine is a story of one who has emerged from the place of obscurity to reveal the life of a true worshiper.

Upon surrendering my life to Christ at the age of nineteen, I jumped, head first, into a life of chasing after God. Even now, I can remember the glorious revelation of touching His Presence the moment that I gave my life to Jesus. I knew, in the inner chambers of my heart, that this experience was the reason for my existence. Even in the early stages of my life in Christ, my soul frequently caught glimpses of the glory of this life of worship. These experiences marked my soul for an ever-unfolding journey to becoming a true worshiper.

At the age of twenty-one, I was invited to move from my then home in Sacramento, California to Portland, Oregon. Even though accepting this offer meant leaving behind everything I knew and all my comforts, I didn't hesitate for one moment. As a zealous young Christ-follower, my soul exploded with joy at the thought of abandoning everything to pursue the life of a laid-down lover of Jesus. Little did I know, the next eight years would be the most lonely, difficult season of my life. I thank God that I can now look back and see that, while unspeakably painful, everything I went through during that time was an integral part of God's plan to fashion me into a true worshiper. Much like David, who was brought up under the harsh leadership of Saul, I found myself under very legalistic and condemning church leadership. Having been relentlessly tormented by the spirit of condemnation, I was desperate just to know that I was loved. This desperation forced me into the place of worship and prayer where I would spend hours at a time searching to catch even a glimpse of God's Presence just to feel His acceptance.

Trust me when I tell you that this season was a "backside of the desert" experience for me. During the late '90s and early 2000s, I had no knowledge of anything that was happening in the church as a whole. I was stuck in my own little world struggling to hold on to my faith, even struggling with the temptation to take my own life. It wasn't that I didn't long for connection with the body of Christ, but I had spent years under the unhealthy, incorrect teaching that I didn't need anything more than God and the Bible. Still again, I look back over these experiences with a heart of gratitude! God knew what He was doing with me just like He knew that the spears being cast at David were developing him into a man after God's own heart.

MY STORY

Was this God's "perfect plan" for my life? I cannot answer that accurately. Such knowledge is just too much for us to grasp. Was it God's perfect plan for the Hebrews to be brutally afflicted by the Egyptians until their cry of suffering finally reached the throne of God? Was it God's perfect plan for six million Jews to be exterminated during World War II before the Allies stepped in and helped Israel to become a nation in 1948? These are all questions that cannot be answered through intellectual understanding. All I can say is that something happens through the suffering of a human soul that produces a desperate, seeking heart that can only be comforted within the throne room of heaven. This is exactly what happened in me during my time in Portland. A life of worship was being developed in the furnace of affliction.

After eight years of living under the heavy hand of condemnation, I finally left this unhealthy environment and found myself in a vicious cycle of drug abuse. I eventually ended up facing ten years of federal prison time. By the grace of God, I served only nine months of a sixteen-month sentence. I can boldly say that this was the best thing that has ever happened to me! It was behind the walls of Folsom Prison where I found true freedom to worship God like I never knew I could. In a tiny chapel with sometimes only five men in attendance, the heavens would open up and the Glory of God would take me into places where flesh and blood cannot go.

For me, worship is so much more than hip songs and trendy church services. Worship is my life source. During the nine months I spent in prison, I learned to abide in the secret place of the Most High God. Through countless hours spent in the place of worship I have discovered an intimacy with God that simply cannot be found elsewhere. His dwelling place has now become my dwelling place. Through worship I have found freedom from years of bitterness and rejection, drug and pornography addiction, fear and insecurity, and the list could go on and on. Whether in a room all by myself or in an auditorium packed with thousands of other worshipers, I now know how to access the realm of heaven. Heaven is so much more than the place we go to when we die. Heaven is God's dwelling place, the place where His Presence dwells with millions of angels worshiping around His throne. Every single person has instant access to this glorious place—we need only to seek Him by faith. Through finding this place in worship, I have become addicted to the Presence of God! Nothing else satisfies but Him.

What follows is a labor of love that has taken me three and one half years to complete. Even as you read, you will see a progression of my own growth through the place of worship. Worship is my life and I now share my life with you just as our Lord Jesus shared His life with us. May my life become an open book to reveal to you the person of Jesus Christ:

> *Father, I pray that these pages will reveal Your heart for a generation. Your heart seeks for worshipers, and may these worshipers arise in this last hour and be on the front lines of the End Time Army that you are revealing Yourself through! Amen*

Part One

TRUE WORSHIP

Chapter 1

THE HEART
OF WORSHIP

But the hour is coming, and now is, when the true worshipers will worship the Father in spirit and truth; for the Father is seeking such to worship Him. God is Spirit, and those who worship Him must worship in spirit and truth (John 4:23-24 NKJV).

How many of us know why we were created? Every one of us has a yearning in our soul to find the purpose of our existence. That yearning has driven many people to achieve beyond what mankind ever thought was possible. Explorers set sail on treacherous seas, discovering new territory and conquering other nations. Others have climbed to the tops of the tallest mountains in the world. Perhaps one of the greatest feats of all was mankind's entrance into outer space, even to walk on the face of the moon.

Yet in all these wonderful accomplishments, I believe that mankind has discovered nothing more than a purpose *for* life, but has fallen quite short of discovering the purpose *of* life. God has placed purpose inside the soul of every human being and, like water in a deep well, that purpose needs to be drawn out.

Let me quickly define the true purpose of our life and existence. The answer that billions of souls since the beginning of time have been looking for can only be found in a personal relationship with the One who created us. Revelation 4:9-11 gives us a vivid picture for what happens continually before the throne of Almighty God. The words of the twenty-four elders around the throne tell us the key that unlocks the purpose of all creation, and the reason of our existence:

The four and twenty elders fall down before him ... and worship him that liveth for ever and ever ... saying, "Thou art worthy, O Lord, to receive glory and honour and power: for thou hast created all things, AND FOR THY PLEASURE THEY ARE AND WERE CREATED" (vv. 10-11 KJV emphasis mine).

As we can see clearly from this key Scripture and from many others that we will look into later, we were created for the purpose of worshipping the Lord God Almighty, and it is in this life of worship that our God takes pleasure in those He created. For the rest of this book, with the help of the Holy Spirit, I will explore what this life of worship entails.

WHAT IS WORSHIP?

Unfortunately, in the church today, when you speak of "worship", the first thing that comes to people's mind is a slow style of music. For some people what comes to mind may be the first part of a church service when every-one sings along and some even lift their hands. We even hear reference to different styles of "worship" which refer to the different styles of music played. Please do not get me wrong; music does play a huge part in the life of worship. There is much scriptural evidence of its importance. There is even a whole book in the Bible called Psalms which literally translated is "songs", but worship is so much more! To get an understanding of worship, we must intimately know the God who created us, the One who formed us, shaped us, and fashioned according to His great love.

Jesus told the woman at the well,

You worship what you do not know; we know what we worship, for

THE HEART OF WORSHIP

salvation is of the Jews. But the hour is coming, and now is, when the true worshipers will worship the Father in spirit and truth; for the Father is seeking such to worship Him. God is Spirit, and those who worship Him must worship in spirit and truth (John 4:22-24 NKJV).

The truth that Jesus was revealing to this woman is what has always been in the Father's heart. God longs for intimacy with His children whom He created. It has always been His desire to reveal Himself to us. In the beginning, God walked and talked with Adam and Eve in the garden of Eden. Before sin entered into the world, man was able to dwell in the fullness of God's Presence and give Him the glory and worship that He is worthy to receive. Scripture tells us in Psalm 8:4-6,

What is man that you are mindful of him, and the son of man that You visit him? For You have made him a little lower than the angels, and You have crowned him with glory and honor. You have made him to have dominion over the works of Your hands; You have put all things under his feet (NKJV).

The Lord created man and clothed him in His own glory. Because of this he was free to look upon the face of God in all His glory and bow before Him in worship. In fact, the Hebrew word for worship is "hawah" which literally means "to bow down, to do obeisance." It alludes to an act of respect before one's superior and essentially signifies submission. Those who used this mode of salutation fell upon their knees and touched the ground with their foreheads. Now let us take a look into its Greek counterpart, "proskyneo," which is defined almost exactly the same as the Hebrew; the interesting key is that the literal translation of this word is "to kiss"—which alludes to physical intimacy.[1]

Worship, from the purest biblical definition, I believe only occurs in the manifest Presence of God which has become available to all humanity in the revelation of Jesus Christ. The term "revelation" simply means "to reveal or unveil". Colossians 2:9 says, *"For in him [Christ] dwelleth all the fullness of the Godhead bodily" (KJV)*. It also says in Colossians 1:15-19:

> *[Christ] Who is the image of the invisible God, the firstborn of every creature: For by him were all things created, that are in heaven, and that are in earth, visible and invisible ... all things were created by him, and for him: And he is before all things, and by him all things consist. And he is the head of the body, the church: who is the beginning, the firstborn from the dead; that in all things He might have the preeminence. FOR IT PLEASED THE FATHER THAT IN HIM SHOULD ALL FULLNESS DWELL (KJV emphasis mine).*

Everything that we desire to know about God is revealed in the person of Jesus Christ. The infinite, God chose to reveal Himself to us through His Son. We do not encounter His Presence through following a set of rules, but through personal relationship with the Son of God, Jesus Christ. It is as Jesus begins to open our eyes in this relationship that true worship will become our way of life.

Jesus says in John 14:21:

> *He who has My commandments and keeps them, it is he who loves Me. And he who loves Me will be loved by My Father, and I will love him and MANIFEST Myself to him"* (NKJV emphasis mine).

We must understand that there is a difference between the omnipresence of God and His manifest Presence. Israel, when they were in the wilderness, had the cloud by day and the fire by night abiding continually above the tent of meeting. For them this was evidence that God's Presence was with them. Yet there were times when the glory of God manifested among them and brought terror into their hearts, and we read that they all fell face down before the Lord in worship. Again, I will say that worship is not something we do from within ourselves, but it is the only natural response to the unveiling of God's Presence. Today, we who believe in the Lord Jesus Christ are assured that the Holy Spirit abides within every one of us. His Presence is continually with us. God Himself says, *"Never will I leave you; never will I forsake you" (Hebrews 13:5)*. The Holy Spirit is God's promise to all who give themselves wholly to Him. He is our helper and our very present help in time of need. Yet, for all those who truly hunger for more of God and have a deeper yearning in their soul to touch Him, He will manifest His glory. Those who long for His manifest Presence are the ones who will experience the worship and intimacy with the Father that Jesus died on the Cross and rose again for us to have. These are the worshipers that the Father is seeking for Himself.

THE WORSHIPER'S HEART

Everything that God has done since the fall has been centered around His plan of redemption: the giving of the Torah through Moses, the sin offerings, the promised Son of David and all the writings of the prophets. These all pointed to the coming of the Messiah, and His death and resurrection that would bring redemption through His blood to all nations, not just Israel. His plan has always been to redeem sinful man! There is a sound that proceeds out of the hearts of the redeemed that gets God's attention. The heart of a worshiper walks in the revelation of what Christ has redeemed them from. It has utter dependence upon God and walks fully aware that Christ in us is the hope of glory, and apart from Him we can do nothing. I write these words to you as someone who has been redeemed from the pit of destruction, not just a researcher of this topic. I share my heart with you as someone who has pressed past the forces of hell to reach the feet of Jesus and worship Him.

In Luke 7:36-50, we read the story of a sinful woman that came with an expensive alabaster jar of perfume. She stood weeping behind Jesus with her tears falling upon His feet. This woman then wiped Jesus' feet with her hair, kissed them, and poured out the perfume on them. Although Luke does not mention this woman's name, we can look at John 12:1-8, which tells of a very similar account and identifies the woman as Mary of Bethany. Though we cannot prove these to be the same incident, I believe that we can glean from them both in the same inspiration of what the Spirit is saying.

In Luke's account we see that the Pharisee who was hosting this gathering for Jesus began to make judgments in his heart against this act of worship. Jesus, knowing his thoughts, tells a parable:

Two men owed money to a certain moneylender. One owed him five hundred denarii, and the other fifty. Neither of them had the money to pay him back, so he forgave the debts of both. Now which of them will love him more?" Simon replied, "I suppose the one who had the bigger debt forgiven." "You have judged correctly," Jesus said. Then He turned toward the woman and said to Simon, "Do you see this woman? I came into your house. You did not give me any water for my feet, but she wet my feet with her tears and wiped them with her hair. You did not give me a kiss, but this woman, from the time I entered, has not stopped kissing my feet. You did not put oil on my head, but she has poured perfume on my feet. Therefore, I tell you, her many sins have been forgiven—as her great love has shown. But whoever has been forgiven little loves little." Then Jesus said to her, "Your sins are forgiven" (Luke 7:41-48 NIV).

In verse 47, Jesus makes a very bold and profound statement. He says, *"Therefore, I tell you, her many sins have been forgiven, for she loved much. But he who has been forgiven little loves little."* This statement has always baffled me. Is it possible for some to love God more than others? Can two people who have equally surrendered their lives to Jesus have different levels of love in their heart for God? If this is so, how is that love measured? We can't find this out until we understand the use of this word "love" in this Scripture. According to the Vines Greek Dictionary, there are two different Greek words for the one verb "love" in our English language. One word is "phileo", which simply means "tender affection" and can also signify the kindness that one person shows to another. The other Greek word is "agapeo" or "agape" which is, in the most direct form, "To express the essential nature of God."2 In this passage, Jesus is stating that the love expressed here is "agape" love. In this act of worship, this woman in Luke 7 was expressing the very nature of God. It was a kind of love that does not exist inside of the human heart, a selfless love. Jesus says in John 15:13, *"Greater love has no one than this, than to lay down one's life for his friends"* *(NKJV)*. The "agape" love can only come from the Father. Romans 5:5 tells us, *"The love of God [agape] has been poured out in our hearts by the Holy Spirit who has been given to us" (NKJV).*

This woman's act of worship GOT GOD'S ATTENTION! Even though she walked in the very depths of sin and darkness, she responded to the Presence of God *by faith*. Hebrews 11:6 tells us, *"Without Faith it is impossible to please God, because anyone who comes to Him must believe that he exists and that he rewards those who earnestly seek him."* Faith always results in action. James 2:26 says, *"For as the body without the spirit is dead, so faith without works is dead also."* I cannot tell you how many times I have questioned in my heart how, during a powerful church service when the Presence of God falls like a blanket, many people walk away complaining. I have personally heard complaints after a move of God such as "I wish the Pastor would do this," or "I wish we could have had this song or that song". These people altogether missed what God had to give them because they did not respond to the Presence of God in faith.

We see this in Luke 7 with this woman and Simon the Pharisee. Simon was sitting in the Presence of God in the flesh, yet he sat criticizing the way Jesus did things. Yet this sinner woman responds to the Presence of God by faith. Her response so touched the heart of God that, I believe, He imparted His very nature into her. She received, in that instant, forgiveness of her many sins and, to fill that deep void that sin once occupied, God imputed His "agape" love. Romans 5:20-21 tells us,

God's law was given so that all people could see how sinful they were. But as people sinned more and more, God's wonderful grace became more abundant. So just as sin entered into all people and brought them to death, now God's wonderful grace rules instead, giving us right standing with God and resulting in life through Jesus Christ our Lord (NLT).

Those who have a deeper need receive more of God's grace to sustain them. His love was then flowing from the heart that was once darkened through sin. God found Himself the kind of true worshiper in this woman that He earnestly desires and seeks after. Religious people will always complain about the extravagant worship that comes from those who give more of themselves at the feet of Jesus.

We see this exact situation in the extravagant worship of Mary of Bethany. When she poured out her offering before the Lord, some of the disciples complained in the same way, saying it was too much! In fact, Mary is also known in Scripture as the one who sat at the feet of Jesus while Martha, her sister, was busied about with service. Mary desired to be as close to Jesus as possible, more than to be busied about in ministering to others. Martha even complained to the Lord about her sister sitting at His feet. Jesus responded to Martha with a loving rebuke. He told her that Mary had chosen the better part that would not be taken away from her (see Luke 10:41-42). Many times the true worshipers will be mocked and ridiculed for their desperate willingness to throw everything aside and minister to the Lord without restraints. Please do not get me wrong; I am not advocating laziness or disorderly conduct. I am simply stating that there are times that we must discern when the Spirit of God is drawing us into His dwelling place for an intimate time of worship. A heart of worship will always be willing to throw caution to the wind to spend time with the lover of their soul.

The woman in Luke 7 and Mary of Bethany are beautiful examples of extravagant worshipers. I don't believe it is by any coincidence that the most unlikely sinful woman and Mary of Bethany have become noted together as the most intimate worshipers in the New Testament. Whether these two women are the same does not matter. What matters is their extreme heart to worship the Lord in a manner that got heaven's attention! This is the heart of worship – *to get heaven's attention!*

Is this your sole desire? Are you seeking after God as if for lost treasure? If Jesus were standing before you, would you be willing to throw caution to the wind no matter how angry those around you became? If you have been redeemed by the blood of Christ, then you are well on your way to receiving this heart of worship. The Father is seeking for true worshipers, and true worshipers are seeking only for Him!

A MAN AFTER GOD'S OWN HEART

There are so many examples in the Word of God of individuals who lived in worship to the Lord. The more we study the lives of these men and women of God, the more we will begin to see a mirror of how we should live in whole-hearted devotion to manifesting God through our life of worship.

There is one man in Scripture that stands out among them all (besides Jesus, of course). I say this for one simple reason: God is the One who chose him to stand out as such! In 1 Samuel 13:14, Samuel tells King Saul, *"The Lord has sought for Himself a man after His own heart" (NKJV)*. This man was David.

Do we truly understand that God is seeking after us much more than we seek after Him? 2 Chronicles 16:9 tells us, *"For the eyes of the Lord range throughout the Earth to strengthen those whose hearts are fully committed to Him."* Psalm 14:2 says, *"The Lord looks down from heaven on the sons of men to see if there are any who understand, any who seek God."* In the garden of Eden, God came looking for Adam, and we even hear His heart cry "Adam, where are you?" Jesus declares to us, *"For the Son of Man is come to seek and to save that which was lost" (Luke 19:10 KJV)*. Lastly, we can look at our key Scripture John 4:23, *"The true worshipers ... are the kind of worshipers the Father seeks."*

What is it that God is looking for? What is it about David's life that got God's attention? The best way to see this is to look at David's life in comparison to the life of King Saul. In 1 Samuel 13, Samuel gives this prophetic word to Saul about God seeking a man after His own heart, after he had failed to keep the specific instruction given to him.

The Philistines had gathered with a great army of thirty thousand chariots, six thousand horsemen, and people as numerable as the sand of the seashore in multitude. Saul had only three thousand trembling men at his side and was losing some of them as they began hiding in caves and thickets, and in rocks and holes. Some even crossed over the Jordan and got as far away as they could from what looked like a sure slaughter. Saul was given very specific instruction through the prophet Samuel. He was instructed to wait in Gilgal for seven days until Samuel came to offer burnt offerings to the Lord and then he would get further instruction. Saul did *almost* all of what Samuel told him and waited in Gilgal but fell short of the full seven days. He began to look around at the fearful and trembling men, and in his own fear he decided to take matters into his own hands and offered up the burnt offering, which was only lawful for the priests to do under God's law. Then, right after he finished this disobedient offering to the Lord, Samuel appeared!

Let's learn from this situation. God is always on time; He is never late! It would be wise for us to get our "spiritual clocks" set on His time. There will be seasons that we will walk through in life that we will wonder if God will ever show up, in the same way Saul did. Then there will be other times that God will be asking for instant response from us while we wait around in procrastination, convincing ourselves that we need to pray about it more. God does not do this to play games with us, He does this to build HIS character within us. Everything that God does, He does for *His* purposes and *His* plans. Those who love Him and are fully committed to Him live completely submitted to this truth.

God's plan for Saul, as it is for all of us after being saved and separated from the world, is to work the Cross through us. For some of you, that may have just caused red flags to go up inside of you. You might be saying, "Wait a minute, the Cross was not introduced until the New Testament, how can you be saying that God had to work the Cross through Saul?" One thing we must understand is that everything from Genesis to Revelation points to Jesus and the Cross. Jesus has always been *"The Lamb slain from the foundation of the world" (Revelation 13:8).* Paul gives us in 1 Corinthians 10:1-10 Old Testament examples to reveal New Testament truth. He then tells us, in verse 11, *"All these things happened to them as examples, and they were written for our admonition, upon whom the ends of the ages have come" (NKJV).* The writer of Hebrews also teaches us, *"For*

THE HEART OF WORSHIP

the law, having a shadow of things to come and not the very image of the things" (Hebrews 10:1 NKJV). We must always read Scripture through the eyes of the Holy Spirit within us, who will always point us in the direction of Jesus and the Cross. The Cross is the central point of all that God is doing on the earth.

God's plan for Saul was to work *His* cross within him. No one is exempt from this process. Even though Saul was given "another heart" (1 Samuel 10:9), he was unyielding to God's continual working within his heart where "old things pass way and all things become new" (see 2 Corinthians 5:17). This is a picture for all of us! When we are born again, God gives every man a "new heart" and a "new mind." He crowns us as children of the King, yet the only way to draw closer to God is through the Cross. Situations in life will arise that will press us on every side. Life will sometimes throw everything at us and bring us to our breaking point. Yet, it is in these circumstances that God gives us His Grace to purify our hearts through the fiery trials that come upon us (James 1:2-4; 1 Peter 1:6-9). Unfortunately, Saul did not understand this. In his time of testing, he disobeyed the Word of the Lord and was rebuked by Samuel, the prophet of God, who said to him,

> *You have done foolishly. You have not kept the commandment of the Lord your God, which He commanded you. For now the Lord would have established your kingdom over Israel forever. But now your kingdom should not continue. THE LORD HAS SOUGHT FOR HIMSELF A MAN AFTER HIS OWN HEART, and the Lord has commanded him to be commander over His people, because you have not kept what the Lord has commanded you!* (1 Samuel 13:13-14 NKJV emphasis mine).

This man was David.

If there was anyone in all the Scriptures who was an example for us as a true worshiper, it was David. As a young boy, he was a lowly shepherd tending the flocks of his father, Jesse. It was in this time that David acquired such an intimacy with the Lord that he was marked by God to

25

be ruler of His people. Even during the time of intense warfare for Israel, David was writing love songs to the Lord out in the fields. During one of the darkest hours in the history of Israel, David's devotion to the Lord and his unrestrained worship of God brought revival to his nation. God found Himself a man who could be trusted with His very heart.

When we look at the comparison between David and Saul, I believe we can grasp revelation that will reveal the heart of God to us. We can see through these first two kings of Israel a pattern for our own lives in pursuing a heart after God's. There are many, upon being born again, that continue in the ways of the world, never surrendering to the Cross and the work of the Holy Spirit. Then there are those who are truly born of the Spirit and instantly forsake the desires of the sinful nature and pursue intimacy with God with every waking breath. the first being Saul, the second being David.

In 1 Samuel 15:17, Samuel spoke to Saul by the Word of the Lord, *"When you were little in your own eyes, were you not head of the tribes of Israel? And did not the Lord anoint you king over Israel?" (NKJV)*. This word was spoken as the Lord was rejecting Saul as king. Somewhere, as happens with many of us, Saul lost the burning passion for God that once motivated his life. He lost the humility that God saw in him which qualified him for promotion.

Jesus makes a statement in Matthew 23:12, *"Whoever exalts himself will be humbled, and he who humbles himself will be exalted" (NKJV)*. Those who walk in humility before the Lord will see promotion in their lives and ministries. Yet, we must understand that promotion is not a license to cast off the humility that exalted us higher! I have told a number of people that I have seen placed into leadership positions this very principle: "Do not lose the humility that God sees in you, now that He has promoted you into a position of leadership." It is a temptation from the enemy to convince ourselves that it is by some "good thing" that we have done that has brought promotion. We all need to be aware of the devil's devices and strategies! Pride and arrogance are the reasons that satan was thrown out of heaven. This is a real danger that we must be aware of. I say this as one who has fallen prey to this attitude. Never lose the one burning desire in your heart to love God with

THE HEART OF WORSHIP

all your soul in order to chase position or notoriety amongst fellow believers. It is in that instant that we lose the heart of worship.

David, on the other hand, as a young man (most scholars say between fourteen to sixteen years old), was anointed to be the next king of Israel by Samuel (1 Samuel 16). Yet, never did he forsake his heart for God by his conduct or his character. Nor did he dishonor King Saul even when Saul was chasing him down to take his life. Never did he attempt to exalt himself as king though God Himself anointed him as such! David was called a "man after God's own heart" and with that heart after God, he was able to recognize, no matter how hard the circumstances of his life, that God was still in control. Over and over we see that David "inquired of the Lord" in difficult situations.

If David was a man chasing after position, he could have taken matters into his own hands. Twice he had the opportunity to take King Saul's life and the kingdom that God declared was rightfully his. But the heartbeat within David would never allow him to do anything that would jeopardize his relationship with God. His pure motivation in life was to do what is pleasing in the sight of His Lord.

David was also a man, like Saul, that made terrible mistakes. In fact, they were much worse than Saul's. Yet David was a man whose heart never lost sight of his utter devotion to God, and he instantly repented. I believe had Saul truly repented for his sin, he could have kept the kingdom. Saul confessed in 1 Samuel 15:24-25, *"I have sinned. I violated the Lord's command and your instruction...Now I beg you, forgive my sin and come back with me, so that I may worship the Lord."* Only God knows what is truly inside the hearts of men. There is nothing hidden from the eyes of the Lord. Samuel replies, *"I will not go back with you. You have rejected the Word of the Lord, and the Lord has rejected you as king over Israel!"* (1 Samuel 15:26). Samuel then turns away from Saul to leave, and Saul reaches out and lays hold of the prophet's robe and it rips. Saul replies to Samuel, revealing the true motive of his heart, *"I have sinned. But please honor me before the elders of my people and before Israel; come back with me, so that I may worship the Lord your God."* Saul says, "The Lord YOUR God." Never once in the life of Saul do we see him call the Lord HIS God. His relationship with God was secondary to his position as king. He was willing to compromise his relationship with God in order to keep his title and right standing with the people.

How many ministers today have we seen compromise in the same fashion! God will always give place for repentance. Let us get this! God will always confront us for our sin, yet His heart is to bring us back into right relationship with Him. The devil will always attempt to pervert the character of God in our eyes. The judgment of God is always executed through His nature of love. When confronted for our sin by the Holy Spirit, either in our personal prayer closet, or by a man or woman of God, or by any means that God pleads with us, His heart is always calling us to repent and change our ways. It is not to beat us over the head or to condemn us. Yet pride will always attempt to raise its ugly head up in our hearts. We can so easily justify ourselves and refuse to repent. The devil will even make us believe that the conviction we are feeling is from him (the devil) in an attempt to make us feel guilty. We might even make excuses before God in our own hearts. Sin is deceitful, and if we do not instantly repent, it will take root. Unfortunately, it is so easy for us to continue with that sin in our hearts, deceiving ourselves. Being right in our own eyes, we have now compromised our relationship with God. Even though Saul did keep the kingdom for a few more years, we see a downward spiral of his character. He chased David, the chosen man of God, to take his life. He killed eighty-five priests of the Lord with the sword (1 Samuel 22). Then, at the end of his life, when he could no longer hear the voice of the Lord, he inquired through a witch (or a medium) to find his way. It was this act of dabbling with the dark arts that Scripture says is the reason that God took Saul's life (1 Chronicles 10:13-14).

David, on the other hand, committed adultery and killed the husband of the woman he committed adultery with. When confronted by the prophet of God for this sin, David instantly repented. David understood the severity of his sin and completely humbled himself in the sight of God. Psalm 51 is a Psalm David wrote after he was confronted by Nathan for his sin. David's pure motivation for his repentance was to keep his relationship with God. David says, *"Create in me a pure heart, O God, and renew a steadfast spirit within me. DO NOT CAST ME FROM YOUR PRESENCE or take your Holy Spirit from me. Restore to me the joy of your salvation and grant me a willing spirit, to sustain me" (Psalm 51:10-12 emphasis mine).* He continues on in verse 15, *"O Lord, open my lips, and my mouth will declare your praise."* This is the heart of a worshiper. His only fear was losing the heart of worship within him.

David, as a king, attained a renown that surpassed all the kings of the earth. He never compromised his heart for God to save himself or his kingdom. Even when Absalom his son attempted to take his throne, David did not fight to keep it. He knew God had given him the throne, and that if He wanted him to remain on it, He would fight for him. In the face of adversity, David always gave glory to God and trusted in Him. Let us learn from a man whom God Himself called a man after His own heart.

WHAT IS IN YOUR HEART?

Jesus makes a statement in Revelation 2:4 to the church at Ephesus. He says, *"Nevertheless, I have this against you, that you have left your first love" (NKJV).* The Lord says this after first commending them for all the good they were doing for His name. Yet, somewhere along the way they lost the heart of worship and left their first love.

This can easily happen to so many of us. We can busy ourselves with so many things, believing we are pleasing God as Saul did, yet lose the burning passion for God in our heart that is truly what pleases God most.

Mary chose the better part, David was willing to throw it all away to keep the heart of God. What kind of heart is in you?

Chapter 2

WHO DO YOU WORSHIP?

You shall have no other gods before me. You shall not make for yourself an idol in the form of anything in heaven above or on the earth beneath or in the waters below. You shall not bow down to them or worship them; for I, the Lord your God, am a jealous God (Exodus 20:2-4).

December 2, 2005 was a day that everything began to change for me. As I sat in a cell in the Sacramento County jail, I was told that I may be facing up to ten years federal prison time. I sat all alone, hopeless, and absolutely broken inside. Along with this grim reality, my physical body was also in extreme pain because I was detoxing from over two years of running hard on methamphetamine and alcohol abuse. Completely alone and broken, I began turning my heart back toward Jesus. Even now I can remember the pain I felt in my heart because I was facing the consequences of all the foolish choices I had made since I had fallen away from the Lord. I knew that my actions were deserving of much more than just ten years federal prison. I knew that I had continually rejected the Lord and I finally saw that my choices had hurt His heart. I was absolutely broken inside.

One of my greatest battles in this moment was the years of strict teaching that God will punish us for our sins. It had been engrafted into my thinking that if I reject God He will reject me. In other words, His acceptance of me was totally based on my performance. If I did good, He loved me. If I wasn't doing good, He didn't love me. It was that black and white. Does this sound familiar to anybody? This was my belief at the core of my being. I had also been taught vehemently that once someone walked away from God after walking with Him in all His goodness, they would lose their salvation and could never get it back. After all, isn't this what the Bible says? I believed what I was taught and I held on to this teaching even to my own demise.

So, with all this teaching engrafted into my thinking, I lay in my cell weeping on my bed. My own belief in the God that I had been taught about condemned me to hell forever! It was in this tormented state that I came to the resolve that even if I spent life in prison, it meant nothing in the scope of eternity away from God. I wept and wept for two days straight, telling God how sorry I was. During this two-day period, my soul touched the grief in His heart towards me. In this state, I cried out, "God, if I have to spend twenty-five years in prison, I don't care. I don't want to spend one more day without you. I want you in my life. I'm sorry, I'm so sorry!"

Though God did not answer me with an audible voice, He sent my grandma to me the next day. She came and told me that she'd had a dream the night before that I had given my life back to the Lord. The Spirit fell upon me right there and joy flooded my soul. As my grandma and I talked about the Lord my heart was revived! Then, immediately after that visit, the chaplain of the jail visited me and gave me a Bible. I began reading it every waking moment. In the secret places of my heart, where I formerly had no desire for God, I was now longing and hungering for Him with all my heart. I knew God had heard my prayer and answered it by giving me a renewed hunger inside for His Presence. I was alive with a fresh zeal to pursue Him with all my being.

From this whole experience I have learned a very important truth that I share in the following two chapters. The Lord is the object of our worship, but true worship only flows from the place of true revelation. For years my relationship with God was only based on holding onto truths that others taught me. Though I had multiple encounters with God in my time alone with Him, I still only worshipped Him according to how I believed Him in my own mind.

Jesus explained to the woman at the well, *"You Samaritans worship what you do not know; we worship what we do know ...* Jesus goes on to say, *"Yet the time is coming and has now come when the true worshipers will worship the Father in spirit and truth, for they are the kind of worshipers the Father seeks. God is Spirit, and His worshipers must worship in spirit and in truth"* (John 4:22-24). There is a truth here that we all must get! The Samaritan people (as is the truth with many today) worshiped what they believed to be the God of Abraham, Isaac, and Jacob, the one true God. With sincere hearts they attempted to worship Him, yet Jesus came with a gripping truth; *they did not even know what they were worshiping.*

THE WORSHIP OF IDOLS

The apostle Paul revealed this truth to the Athenians in Acts 17: they were worshipping a god that they did not know. As he walked around, he saw the whole city given over to idols. For this reason he began to preach to them and said:

> *"Men of Athens, I perceive that in all things you are very religious [KJV superstitious], for as I was passing through and considering the THE OBJECTS OF YOUR WORSHIP, I even found an altar with this inscription: To the unknown God. Therefore, the One whom you worship without knowing, Him I proclaim to you. God, who made the world and everything in it, since He is Lord of heaven and earth, does not dwell in temples made with hands. Nor is He worshiped with men's hands ... also for in Him we live and move and have our being, as some of your own poets have said, 'For we are also His offspring'. Therefore, since we are the offspring of God, we ought not to think that the Divine Nature is like gold or silver or stone, something shaped by art and man's devising. Truly, these*

times of ignorance God overlooked, but now commands all people everywhere to repent, because He has appointed a day on which He will judge the world in righteousness by the Man whom He has ordained [Jesus]. He has given assurance of this to all by raising Him from the dead" (Acts 17:22-31 NKJV emphasis mine).

There is something here that I believe many people don't understand or perceive. This may be offensive to some, but it is the truth nonetheless. If our worship is not founded upon the truth of what God has revealed through the Holy Scripture, then it is unto a "god" that we have created in our own minds, according to our own limited understanding. In Exodus 20, God gave the famous Ten Commandments; the first two say this:

"I am the Lord your God, who brought you out of Egypt, out of the land of slavery. You shall have no other gods before me. You shall not make for yourself an image in the form of anything in heaven above or on the earth beneath or in the waters below. You shall not bow down to them or worship them; for I, the Lord your God, am a jealous God" (Exodus 20:2-5).

It is no coincidence that the first two commandments deal directly with the God whom we worship and the importance of our worship of Him. The Lord is the object of our worship, yet we must be very careful not to turn the Lord who created us into an object created from our own perception—a god who fits into our own little box of what we would want a "god" to be like. This is what the Bible calls an "idol."

Because of the existence of sin in the hearts of fallen men and women, people attempt to worship a God that they don't even know, or even better said; they attempt to worship a God whom they can't know. Without the atoning work of Christ and the Cross, people attempt to worship God through sin-tainted lives. People will "make" for themselves a god that fits their lifestyle or culture, or turn Him into a "genie" that is there to give them their every wish. It is for this very reason that there are so many different religions in the world we live in. Every religion believes that they have the way to God and that they see Him clearly. There are also people who believe that all religions are right and that God loves them all and accepts their worship. Even in Christianity, there are multitudes of different denominations of believers who profess their denomination is *the* way.

So who is right? Do we have a Creator God who can only be limited to the way we believe Him to be? Or do we have a God (as many today believe) that just lets everybody believe what they want, and everything will just work itself out in the end? I hope we see that these are legitimate questions that many people struggle with when it comes to putting their faith and trust in God. These are questions that deserve answers! There are many sincere people in the world who desire truth, yet because every human being has an enemy of their soul, truth can be twisted into a lie. We must get that! There is an enemy, called satan, who, since the beginning, has been twisting the truth of God into his perverted lie. His sole desire is to take the worship that belongs to God and receive it to himself.

Satan has walked in the high places of God. He has seen the splendor and glory of God and was even anointed with a high position among the Stones of Fire (Ezekiel 28:12-19). He has seen and was even a leader of the continual worship of God that takes place around His throne. Isaiah says this,

> *How you are fallen from heaven, O Lucifer, son of the morning! How you are cut down to the ground, you who weakened the nations! For you have said in your heart: "I will ascend into heaven, I will exalt my throne above the stars of God; I will also sit on the mount of the congregation on the farthest sides of the north; I will ascend above the heights of the clouds, I will be like the Most High." Yet you shall be brought down to Sheol [Hell], to the lowest depths of the Pit* (Isaiah 14:12-15 NKJV).

Somehow Lucifer allowed envy and jealousy to enter into his heart. He was in the midst of the paradise of God, in the place of perfection, yet somehow sin crept into his heart because of jealousy towards the worship that God receives continually in heaven. Satan set out in his heart to be "like the Most High." His motives have not changed—he still lusts after the worship that belongs to God alone. My purpose in writing this is not to lift satan up or give him undue attention, but as the apostle Paul admonishes, *"...in order that satan might not outwit us. For we are not unaware of his schemes"* *(2 Corinthians 2:11)*. If our worship is not devoted to the true God, then satan is being glorified! There is no middle of the road. You are either a partaker of the kingdom of God, or you are a slave to the kingdom of darkness.

How many people today realize that as human beings *we will worship something*! We have already read that we were created for worship, yet just because we are not bowing down physically to some figure we've carved out of stone does not mean that we don't have "idols" in our hearts. There is a place in the soul of every human being that longs for intimacy with our Creator. Because of this, whatever we begin to worship and adore other than God alone will become our idol. We all have a deep longing inside to be loved and to give love to others. For many, this is the driving force behind many life pursuits, especially when it is the love between a man and a woman. People even make statements such as "he worships the ground she walks on." Yet there is the deepest inward part of every man, woman, and child that can only be satisfied by a personal love relationship with the Father who created us to be loved and to love Him with all our heart, soul, mind, and strength. Worship belongs to God alone. But when we give preeminence to anything in our hearts above God, it is in that moment it becomes an idol.

I am very aware that there have been many religious fanatics that have brought this truth to a very legalistic lifestyle and say, "You can't love or enjoy anything in life but God." Pushing this kind of religious lifestyle brings people under bondage to guilt and depression that comes straight from the pit of hell! This type of lifestyle can't be any farther from the truth. God has also created us to enjoy all His creation and we are to enjoy the life that He has given to us—*but with all things in their right place*. Yet again, because of the existence of sin in the hearts of men and women, satan will pervert this truth as well. This is the very reason it is so important that we pursue a heart after God upon being born again! When we live with a heart that burns for God, we will not secretly house other lovers in our hearts. It will not feel like a "duty" or that we "have to" love God, but there will be a deep out-flowing of passion that longs to please God and "wants" to love and worship Him. A heart that burns in love for Him is the most powerful weapon against allowing the object of worship to be anything other than a personal relationship with the Lord who loves us perfectly.

THERE WERE "TWO TREES"

Satan will always attempt to pervert our knowledge of God. How we perceive God in our hearts and minds is everything. That is why we must fight for that place of worship. The apostle Paul says in 2 Corinthians 10:4-5,

> *For the weapons of our warfare are not carnal but mighty in God to the pulling down of strongholds, casting down arguments and every high thing that exalts itself against the KNOWLEDGE OF GOD, bringing every thought into captivity to the obedience of Christ* (NKJV emphasis mine).

Satan's tactics have not changed since the garden; just as he perverted the character of God in the eyes of Eve, he will do the same with each of us. God is love, and all His commands proceed from His heart of love. Our God is not a cruel and demanding tyrant but a wise and loving Father. All His commands are not given to bind us under rules but to establish boundaries in our loving relationship with Him.
Genesis 2:16-17 says,

> *And the Lord commanded the man, "You are free to eat from any tree in the garden; but you must not eat from the tree of the knowledge of good and evil, for when you eat from it you will surely die."*

God gave freely of everything He made that we might enjoy and take pleasure in the works of His hands. Yet God still gave "commands" to us, not to bind us or to keep something good from us, but for our protection!

One of the most powerful truths about God that must be established in our hearts is that He is good. Everything He does is done in His nature of love. Our faith and trust must be founded upon the Rock of who God is by nature. God is love and He is good. If we are not founded upon the truth that we are loved and that He is good, then we will become offended and fall when the tempter comes, just as Eve fell prey to his deceptions.

Let's listen to what satan says to Eve in Genesis 3:1, *"Did God really say, 'You must not eat from any tree in the garden?.'"* Look at how subtle satan was. He twisted the Word of God just enough to pervert God's loving command into the appearance of a binding restriction. It was in that moment that everything she knew to be true about God was instantly shaken. Had she been rooted and grounded in love for God and in close communion with Him, she could have regained the upper hand by remembering God's goodness. Look at her response to the serpent, *"We may eat fruit from the trees in the garden* [it almost seems like she is trying to convince herself. When we are not founded upon who God is, we will become confused by the devil's attacks, much like venom from a serpent confuses the blood stream], *but God did say, 'You must not eat fruit from the tree that is in the middle of the garden, and you must not touch it, or you will die.'"*

There are two things in Eve's response that reveal error that must be addressed for us to learn from. First of all, as most people clearly see, God never said not to "touch" the Tree of Knowledge of Good and Evil. Some people speculate that perhaps she only received this command from her husband and never received it by revelation from the Lord for herself. I do believe that is a strong possibility; yet I also believe that it is possible, even if she did receive this command by revelation directly from the Lord, that in this moment of temptation, satan would still be able to pervert God's character in Eve's eyes.

I will give you a New Testament example to back this in John the Baptist. John clearly heard the word of the Lord concerning Jesus and even declared Him to be "The Lamb of God". He was later thrown into prison and walked through probably the roughest trial of his life. During this trial, he sent his disciples to Jesus to ask Him if He was the One to come. Jesus responded by instructing John's disciples to tell him all that they had

WHO DO YOU WORSHIP?

seen and finished off with this statement, *"Blessed is he who is not offended in Me"* (see Matthew 11:6). So we see that John, in his moment of weakness, was unable to grasp truth that had clearly been revealed by the Spirit.

Life will often bring moments when it feels as if all hell is breaking loose against you. Everything can fall apart all at once and the first thing the enemy will attempt to do in these moments is convince us that, "God doesn't care. If He cared, why would He allow this?" The worst thing to do in these crossroad moments is to partner with satan's lies and become offended at God or blame Him. It is true that in these moments, everything we know about God (His loving and merciful nature) all come into question. Yet it can be these moments that define us!   Job lost all of his wealth and even all his children in one instant. *Yet he chose to fall on his face and worship God* and said, *"'The Lord gives and the Lord takes away, but blessed be the name of the Lord'. In all this Job did not sin by charging God with wrongdoing"(Job 1:21-22).* What Job said here was not even "theologically" correct. Scripture tells us that it was satan who came before the throne of God and moved upon the Lord to allow this calamity upon Job to test him. This happened after God had just bragged about Job's faithfulness. So Job's response to what took place revealed that his faith was founded upon the goodness of God no matter what. It was not God who took everything away. Job was simply making a faith-filled statement in the midst of confusion and chaos that he was going to worship the Lord.

Now let's get back to Eve. We must remember that this incident took place before sin entered the world. In fact, this is the very occurrence that opened the door for sin to come and reign over all of Adam and Eve's children to this day. When satan came, he perverted everything they knew to be true about God. Yet, even in the confusion, had Eve been firmly rooted in the goodness of God (like we just saw in Job), she could have recognized the doubt and fallen down immediately before God and worshiped Him, finding help in her hour of need. Unfortunately, as we all know, that is not what took place.

The second error I found in Eve's response is something that I had never seen until writing this book. Eve said, *"But God did say, 'you must not eat fruit from the tree that is in the middle of the garden'" (Genesis 3:3). God*

39

never said that! He said not to eat of the Tree of Knowledge of Good and Evil. In fact, *there were two trees in the middle of the garden (Genesis 2:9)!* There was the Tree of Knowledge of Good and Evil and the Tree of Life. WHAT HAPPENED TO THE TREE OF LIFE? The whole time that this scenario was taking place in *"the middle of the garden,"* the Tree of Life was right there also. There were two trees to choose from. There will always be two trees to choose from! God has created us with the power and privilege of making choices and living with the consequences of these choices.

The Lord opened my eyes as He showed me this scenario taking place with the serpent and Adam and Eve at the Tree of Knowledge of Good and Evil. The Tree of Life was there the whole time! It is as if I could hear the voice of the Lord shouting to them saying, "Take, eat of this tree and live forever!" Yet satan was able to pervert the character of God in the eyes of Adam and Eve and make it look as if God was holding something good back from them.

Does that sound familiar? How often do we wrestle with God in our own hearts, lusting after something that will only harm us? Deep down inside we know it is wrong, yet we so easily convince ourselves that if God really were a loving God then He would want us to be happy. Listen to what Scripture says happens next, *"So when the woman saw that the fruit of the tree was good and pleasing to the eye, and a tree desirable to make one wise, she took of its fruit and ate" (Genesis 3:6 NKJV).* Somehow Eve was blinded to the fact that the Tree of Life was right there as well. I believe what blinded her is the same thing that blinds many today as well. 1 John 2:16 talks about "the lust of the flesh, the lust of the eye, and the pride of life".

The key to all this that took place in the garden was that satan was able to take Eve's eyes off of the Lord and put them on herself. *The love of self is the root of the sin nature also called pride.* This is the nature within the devil himself that caused him to fall from the Presence of God. This is the nature that Jesus died on the cross to save us from!

Though Adam and Eve walked in the perfection of God's selfless love, satan tempted Eve to look inward at her "self". *"The serpent said to the woman, 'YOU surely will not die! For God knows that in the day YOU eat from it YOUR eyes will be opened, and YOU will be like God, knowing good from evil" (Genesis 3:4-5 NASB emphasis mine)*. I purposely emphasized the enemy's usage of the word "you" so you can recognize his tactic. When our hearts are not fully fixed upon the Lord in wholehearted devotion and intimacy with Him, we become prey to the enemy's scheme. He will always tempt us to use our knowledge of God to fulfill our own desire. Notice that satan did not tempt Eve with going out to a bar and drinking herself into a stupor. Nor did he tempt her with sleeping with another man other than her husband, nor getting high on drugs (I say this to bring this example into our everyday temptations). Those things Eve never would have fallen for. Again, I will point out that it was called the Tree of Knowledge of Good and Evil.

Most of us today will never be too enticed by the "evil" side of this tree, and satan is cunning enough to know this. But it is very likely that every one of us will be tempted with "good things" that are contrary to the will of God for our lives. This is the trap that the enemy will always set before us, for he knows the selfish nature well. He knows that we can easily set ourselves and our pursuits in life as our biggest idols. Pursuits that are completely harmless can very quickly become the stumbling block that will take many down a path far away from relationship with Christ, if they are not rooted in love and obedience to the will of God,

As we look at the bait that satan set before Eve, we can see this very clearly. He said, *"Your eyes will be opened, and you will be like God, knowing good from evil."* We must realize that this was something that was already given to Adam and Eve at creation. God created them in His image and in His likeness. Had Adam and Eve continued to walk with God and eaten of the Tree of Life, they would have continued to grow in His image and likeness; they would have "been like God". *This was God's will!*

Never should we take matters into our own hands and deliberately disobey the Word of the Lord in pursuit of what God has already promised us. James 1:17-18 tells us,

Every good and perfect gift is from above, coming down from the Father of the heavenly lights, who does not change like shifting shadows. He chose to give us birth through the Word of Truth, that we might be a kind of first fruits of all He created.

God has already provided all things freely, yet when we pursue these things with a covetous heart (even good things) outside of God's provision, then whatsoever we are in pursuit of has become an idol. The Bible tells us that covetousness *is* idolatry (see Colossians 3:5).

Many believers today, without even realizing it, have laid aside their burning heart for God and left their first love in pursuit of things like a wife or a husband, ministry, houses, family, hobbies, favorite pastimes, careers and the list could go on and on. There is nothing inherently sinful about these things but they become sin when they become an object of worship that takes the place of a burning, intimate relationship with Jesus.

PURSUING THE TRUE GOD

I realize that I have hit hard on the issue of worshiping idols. It is very heartbreaking to me (and even more so to the Lord) that many sincere people have fallen prey to this stumbling block. In this day and age there is a kind of spiritual awakening taking place not only in America but around the world. Many people are hungry for something more than what this world has to offer, and in this hunger they are beginning to look for spiritual answers. We must open our eyes to this. Satan knows this as well, and he will do everything he can to bring these hungry souls into the bondage of believing they are free, when in reality they are believing a lie.

Yet, it is in this generation that the kingdom of God and His Christ will also reap the greatest harvest of souls that the world has ever seen. This move of God will be led by an army of worshipers who have laid down their own lives at the Cross in pursuit of an intimate burning relationship with the One True God. As a result of this laid down life, this army of worshipers will walk in the authority and power of the Holy Spirit. These worshipers will tear down the altars of idol worship and again rebuild the altar of the Lord. God Himself will answer with fire. This army of worshipers will reflect the image of the true object of worship into the earth. Let's now move on into looking at this True Object of our worship.

Chapter 3

THE OBJECT
OF OUR AFFECTION

And they sang a mighty chorus: "Worthy is the Lamb who was slaughtered to receive power and riches and wisdom and strength and honor and glory and blessing." And then I heard every creature in heaven and on earth and under the earth and in the sea. They sang: "Blessing and honor and glory and power belong to the one sitting on the throne and to the Lamb forever and ever." And the four living beings ... and the twenty-four elders fell down and worshiped the Lamb (Revelation 5:12-14 NLT).

One of the most beautiful things that I have found to be true about God is that He is past finding out. He will forever be the God who surpasses knowledge. Just when we think we know something about Him, the Lord will break through with fresh revelation of His splendor that leaves us face down in awe and completely wrecked inside. The truth of the matter is that all true worship is birthed from this place of the unveiling of the God who is past finding out. This is where we must lay aside every preconceived ideology of what we thought we knew about the King of Majesty and come, with fear and trembling, before the true object of our worship and affection. The Lord Himself is desirous to reveal His secrets to all those who love His appearing. The Word of God tells us, *"The secret of the Lord is for those who fear Him, and He will make them know His covenant" (Psalm 25:14 NASB).* Before we attempt to understand the object of worship, let us first attempt to grasp and abide in what the Word of God refers to as "the fear of the Lord."

THE FEAR OF THE LORD

The true, healthy fear of the Lord is so desperately needed in the church today. I am by no means claiming to be an expert in understanding what it truly means to fear the Lord, but I will say this: all true worship of the Living God is an outward expression that proceeds from a heart that abides in the fear of the Lord. Proverbs 1:7 tells us, *"The fear of the Lord is the beginning of knowledge,"* and again in Proverbs 9:10, *"The fear of the Lord is the beginning of wisdom, and the knowledge of the Holy One is understanding" (NASB).* So we can see through these two Scriptures that the fear of the Lord is the key that unlocks wisdom and knowledge, and even understanding hinges on our knowledge of the holiness of God, which only comes to those who fear Him.

The word for "beginning" in the Hebrew language is "reshiyth" which means "the first, in place and time, order or rank-beginning, chief, first, principle thing".[1] Considering this, as we begin to explore the true object of worship, we must start where the Word of God instructs us: with the fear of the Lord.

The fear of the Lord is a biblical principle that is rarely discussed in the church today. Perhaps we could venture to say that many teachers avoid this principle because it was severely abused in times past. Some would say that it was a scare tactic used by insecure leaders to gain control over those they were called to lead. It could also just be the simple fact that this value has been neglected in the daily lives of many of today's leaders. Whatever the reason may be, it is imperative that we grasp, from our hearts, what it truly means to walk in the fear of the Lord.

So what does it mean to "fear" the Lord? Is it being afraid of God? I will agree that when the , infinite God, who transcends all His creation, humbles Himself to appear before finite, sinful men, the only natural response

THE OBJECT OF OUR AFFECTION

is fear and trembling. But is that necessarily being afraid of God? We see this with Ezekiel, Daniel, and also John on the isle of Patmos. When Ezekiel had his first encounter with God, he was caught up between heaven and earth and saw "visions of God." When God was through revealing Himself, Scripture tells us that Ezekiel sat astonished by the River Chebar for seven days. What he saw from God so blew away everything he thought he knew that he sat out of commission for seven whole days (see Ezekiel 1).

Daniel was given insight into the prophetic future and he testified that his comeliness was turned into corruption in the Presence of the Holy God. He also stated that after receiving a vision from God, he *"fainted, and was sick for certain days ... and I was astonished at the vision, but none understood it" (Daniel 8:27 KJV).* Lastly, we see another glorious encounter in Revelation. The apostle John heard the resurrected Christ speaking from behind. As he turned to see Him, he beheld His face shining like the sun: His eyes were as a flame of fire, and out of His mouth came a two edged sword. John tells us, *"When I saw Him, I fell at His feet as dead" (Revelation 1:17 KJV).* These glorious encounters give us a picture that it is not always lovey- dovey, fluffy cloud experiences when God deals with men. Oftentimes they are dreadful, fearful revelations that are more than any living man can behold.

We see the first manifestation of fear all the way back in the garden with Adam and Eve.

> *Then the man and his wife heard the sound of the Lord God as He was walking in the garden in the cool of the day, and they hid from the Lord God among the trees of the garden. But the Lord called to the man, "Where are you?" He answered, "I heard you in the garden, and I WAS AFRAID because I was naked; so I hid"* (Genesis 3:8-10 emphasis mine).

Adam and Eve's initial response to the Presence of the Lord was to hide in fear. Fear will oftentimes be our initial response to the manifest Presence of God as long as we live in these mortal bodies. So again, the

45

question: "Is the fear of the Lord being afraid of God?" I believe there is a fine line between being afraid of God and the fear of the Lord. Being "afraid" is a human emotion, which is rooted in the sinful nature, yet the fear of the Lord is rooted in the perfect love of God, which casts out the fear of man. A healthy fear of the Lord begins with the compelling revelation of who He is. The one who is afraid of God has something to hide; the one who fears the Lord will fall face down in worship before Him. The fear of the Lord is a natural response to His glorious Presence. But whether we respond in worship, or are afraid of God, is determined by the condition of our own hearts.

God's Presence will always reveal the true motives of our hearts. Nothing is hidden from Him (see Hebrews 4:12), yet we see Adam and Eve attempting to hide themselves from the Presence of the Lord. They forsook the fear of God and became deceived by believing that they could actually hide from God. This is exactly what happens to those of us who forsake the Lord as the true object of worship, and give our "fear" to lesser objects.

In the church today we often attempt to equate the concept of the fear of the Lord with "reverence." I wholly agree with that as well, yet I do believe that it is important to keep the fear of the Lord as just that—fear! As with other key biblical principles such as the Cross, the blood of Christ, repentance, and hell, we cannot soften these concepts in an attempt to avoid offending people. So also is the concept of the fear of the Lord, it cannot be deduced down to a simple awe or reverence as much as I do believe our God is worthy of these.

There are many things in life that will "awe" people. Most of God's creation will inspire awe, yet we are warned in Scripture (and also by simple common sense) not to worship the creation. Scripture also instructs us to show due reverence to leaders (even double honor to those who labor in the word of God (1 Timothy 5:17), yet we are commanded to worship God alone. There's an old saying that goes like this, "You will serve the one whom you fear," yet I will go even further and say it this way: "The one whom you fear is the one whom you will give your worship to."

When we walk in the fear of the Lord there will be no other that will receive our worship but God alone. Unfortunately, because of the presence of sin in the world, the Lord has had to compete with other so-called "gods". The truth of the matter is that these "gods" are not gods at all. There is only one God and Father of all creation. He is the only One who spoke, and the universe came into being. In fact, He does not need to convince Himself that He is God. He is only known as God to His creation; He revealed Himself by His name "Yahweh", which, to this very day, is such a marvelous name that no one can figure it out! I say this to shed some light on the reality that God is not insecure about who He is. The apostle Paul says this in Romans 3:3-4, *"What if some did not have faith? Will their lack of faith nullify God's faithfulness? Not at all! Let God be true and every human being a liar."* In other words, us putting our faith in God is not what makes Him God! He is forever Him, who is without beginning of days nor end of life (Hebrews 7:3)—*He lives forever!*

I remember back when I was young in the Lord and reading Revelations 10. The apostle John had a vision of a mighty angel coming down from heaven. His face shone like the sun and his legs were like pillars of fire! With one foot he stood on the sea, with the other foot he stood on dry ground. I read this and thought, "WOW! Here is John, who rested his head on the breast of Jesus, one of the great apostles of the Lamb. *He* stands in awe of this huge angelic being that comes down from heaven." What happened next wrecked me: this huge angelic being lifts his right hand to heaven and Scripture says, *"He swore by Him who lives forever and ever, who created the heavens and all that is in them, the earth and all that is in it, and the sea and all that is in it" (Revelation 10:6)*. In this moment I got it! As amazing of an apostle that John was, and as glorious of a being this angel was; *we worship the same God.* The Lord of creation is the only One who inspires holy fear worthy of bowing before. Later on in Revelation 22, John begins to bow before the mighty angel who was speaking to him and the angel rebukes him and tells him to worship God alone!

Life is full of mysteries that human beings, in our finite states, will never fully comprehend. For example, as a young boy I can remember attempting to grasp the concept of "forever." When my parents would tell me that God was never born because He has always existed, my little mind would strain to figure out this mystery. How about the concept that the universe never ends! To be honest, *my little mind still strains to even attempt grasping such wonderful things.* The sad truth is that, to this day, mankind is using all their resources to attain answers that can never be found except through the revelation of the knowledge of God—things simply too wonderful to attain such as the glories and the wonders of the created universe. These are just a glimpse into the revelation of the Living God.

Even with all the magnificent, breathtaking images captured by the Hubble space telescope such as beautiful nebulas, enormous stars which are exponentially larger than our sun; these are only a glimpse to the glory that shall be revealed at His coming! Are you excited about the Lord of Glory yet? Does not His majesty just burn within you making you want to seek His face with an even deeper fervor? *"The heavens declare the glory of God; the skies proclaim the work of His hands" (Psalm 19:1).* When we have a proper image of God, then all we see in creation declares who He is!

Billions of dollars have gone into scientific research to explore the vastness of the created known cosmos, yet in all their searching for answers it has only bred more questions. There is only one answer—*knowing God intimately!* He is the *only* One who spoke and the world came into being. He is the One who measures the universe by the span of His hand. There are unsearchable riches in His Presence; glories that will forever boggle the minds of all who fear the Lord! *"The secret of the Lord is for those who fear Him, and He will make them know His covenant" (Psalm 25:14 NASB).* For those who fear the Lord, He will unlock the door to all the mysteries that have been hidden from the eyes of the wise and prudent.

In one encounter with the Living God, the individual that fears the Lord can receive exponentially more revelation knowledge than during years spent in the most prestigious seminaries and Bible schools. Please do not get me wrong, I am not against education, in fact, I strongly encourage it. Yet knowledge without a heart that fears God is a grave danger to anyone who calls themselves a believer. The fear of the Lord will keep one grounded in the love of God. The reality is that we will all come to revelations of God; it is just a natural part of walking with Him. Those born of the Spirit will have rapturous encounters with the Lord. It is His great pleasure to reveal Himself to us—mysteries which words cannot utter.

I remember one encounter I had with the Lord one evening while lying in bed reading a book. My wife was asleep next to me. I felt the Lord literally take me up into the Spirit and open the vastness of His splendor. For three hours I lay there completely caught up in His glory and in awe of His greatness, yet I trembled in my heart. Something inside of me kept shouting, "I have seen too much!" I had this deep, holy fear that if the Lord let go of me, I would die. The Holy Spirit then said something to me that I will never forget. He said, "To whom much is given, much is required." I knew He was telling me that I was now responsible for what He had shown me and I was to do something with it. A heart that fears God will grasp the urgency of His heart. The Lord does not reveal His knowledge to us just so we can sit back and bask in His glory. As wonderful as this is to a worshiper, this is not the purpose of God in this present age. If our encounters with God do not cause us to be transformed into His very image, thus reflecting His image back into the earth, then we have missed the purpose altogether. The heart that is not founded in the fear of the Lord can easily be lifted up in these encounters and turn to pride.

The apostle Paul gives a perfect illustration of this truth in 2 Corinthians 12. He tells the Corinthian church about a man in Christ who was caught up to the third heaven. Most scholars agree that He was talking about himself. He said that he was given visions and revelations and even heard things expressed in these encounters that were not lawful for him to repeat. He shares in verses 6-7,

> If I wanted to boast, I would be no fool in doing so, because I would be telling the truth. But I won't do it … even though I have received such wonderful revelations from God. So to keep me from becoming proud, I was given a thorn in my flesh, a messenger from Satan to torment me and keep me from becoming proud (NLT).

Paul had multiple encounters with God that are reported in the book of Acts (see Acts 9;16; 23;27), yet on the road to Damascus he did not just sit there in the glory of God that shone as bright as the noon day sun. He sat trembling in the Presence of the Lord and asked, "*What would you have me to do?*" From that day forward Paul walked in the fear of the Lord and lived the rest of his days "obedient to the heavenly vision" (see Acts 26:19). The fear of the Lord will produce in us a life of obedient living. One who fears God will keep the way of the Lord.

The fear of the Lord is the beginning of knowledge and wisdom. It is what will keep us founded upon the truth of God and keep us from sinning against Him by departing from His Presence. The fear of the Lord is not something that is produced from our own hearts. As I said at the beginning; this holy fear is the by-product of an encounter with our holy God. True worship is only produced by a heart that fears the Lord, but I must also say this as I close: worship is not true worship unless it proceeds from a place of burning love for God. There must be a drawing near to Him. The heart that truly fears God loves Him so much that it is simply afraid of living without Him. If we only walk in the fear of the Lord without the end result of burning love that wants to please Him wholly, then we will end up living a life of heartless outward displays of religious rituals that bear no fruit. Yet love devoid of fear results in lawlessness. We can easily begin to make choices that wander away from God when we have no fear of consequences. The fear of the Lord produces worship, and the end result of worship is love for God. *Worship is the key!*

ALL CONSUMING FIRE

Our God is a Consuming Fire (Deuteronomy 4:24; Hebrews 12:29), which devours everything that comes into contact with Him. His Presence emanates with an unquenchable burning. Just ask the seraphim in Isaiah 6! Literally translated "on fire ones" or "burning ones", these angelic beings dwell so close to the Presence of God that all of heaven's hosts look upon them as they burn. The whole multitude in heaven worships day and night before the throne of God, with the twenty-four elders and the cherubim, but only the seraphim have the name the burning ones! How many of us desire to dwell so close to the All Consuming Fire (which is God Himself) that we would just literally burn for Him in worship? Let us wholly give ourselves over as a living sacrifice and allow the fire of His Presence to consume us on the altars before His throne and *just burn!*

To all those who do not walk in the fear of the Lord, I believe that the consuming fire of His Presence will bring terror and dread, as it did to the children of Israel at Mount Sinai. They all beheld as the mountain quaked and burned with fire. Exodus 19:18 says, *"Mount Sinai was covered with smoke, because the Lord descended on it IN FIRE. The smoke billowed up from it like smoke from a furnace, and the whole mountain trembled violently"* (emphasis mine). When the Lord of Glory chose to manifest Himself to His people, *He descended in fire!* So terrifying was the sight to the children of Israel that Scripture tells us, *"They trembled with fear. They stayed at a distance, and said to Moses, 'Speak to us yourself and we will listen. But do not have God speak to us or we will die'"* (Exodus 20:18-19). The fire and the burning terrified the children of Israel so much that they only stood at a distance and begged that they would not have to endure His Presence any longer. The consuming fire *is* God's nature and His Presence burns with holy Fire! Lovers of His Presence will not shrink back in fear but draw near as Moses did!

I believe that the fire of His Presence is related to the emotions of our God. Deuteronomy 4:24 says, *"The Lord our God is a consuming fire, a jealous God."* The Lord has emotions and He desires us with a burning passion. How else would humans have emotions if these were not a reflection of our Creator? His fire comes with His burning passion and jealous love for us. The consuming fire of God is also related to His holiness—*a Holy Fire.* As the seraphim burn in His Presence the only thing that comes out of their mouths is "Holy, Holy, Holy." The fire of God burns them continuously and fills them with a burning passion to worship without restraint. These burning ones are not just singing a song to God like we do in our Sunday morning church services. These worshipers are responding to the holy fire that is burning and consuming every ounce of their being; all they can do is scream out "HOLY." *They are describing what they see!* Oh God, let us see what the seraphim see, let us burn with holy fire!

One cannot enter into the holy fire of God's Presence and not experience transformation. He is a consuming fire, a jealous God, and He will not share our gaze with other lovers. James warns us that if we are friends with the world, then we are the enemies of God. He even goes to the extreme of calling these kind "adulterers and adulteresses", and he goes on to say, *"The Spirit which dwells in us YEARNS JEALOUSLY" (James 4:5 NKJV emphasis mine).* The Spirit of God, which dwells within every believer, fills us with a jealous burning to lead us back to the lover of our souls. Those who are gripped by His burning love and passion will endure the fire of His holiness which will demand we change our ways and lay aside every other lover that can steal our gaze from Him. His holy fire will burn all else away and leave us burning for Him alone.

Having approached the holy fire of God, one cannot help but to acquire a burning heart. Perhaps I can also say it this way; you cannot touch fire and not get burned! When you acquire a heart that burns in love for God, you will always make a choice to draw yet nearer to the consuming fire no matter the cost. You will count all things but loss for the excellency of knowing the One who has captured your heart with passion and fire. Is this not what it is all about? Jesus summed up everything into two great commandments: to love God with everything within us and to love our neighbor as ourselves. When you touch the fire of God you will acquire a burning heart, which is the only necessary key to fulfilling the law of God. Everything that Christ accomplished on the Cross was done to restore that burning love relationship with God and His creation that was lost in the garden.

It is the fire of God's Presence that literally burns away all the impurities in our lives that hinder us from approaching closer to our holy God. When we are gripped by the love of God burning within, we realize that everything burned up in the fire of His holiness was not worth holding onto anyway. In our flesh it is a painful process to let go of everything we once held dear to our lives, but the reward of beholding the beauty of His face is well worth the price. It is in the fire where every motive of the heart is revealed, just as it is in the fire where gold is purified. Every impurity comes up to the surface and is disposed of. For the gold,

THE OBJECT OF OUR AFFECTION

this brings out its purest form; *so it is with us!* Nothing is hidden from His eyes of fire; everything is naked and exposed in the eyes of the God whom we serve (Hebrews 4:12). Every impure motive is dealt with. Are we serving God out of pure devotion and love for Him, or is it only to get His blessing? Are we only serving Him to avoid going to hell? Or are we seeking only to enjoy the benefits of being a child of the King? The fire of God will reveal all!

The simple truth of the matter is that there is not one person on the face of the whole earth whose heart is pure before our holy God. There are so many different motives behind every decision we make in life; a driving force that fuels every action. If we are driven by anything but fiery love for God there will not be fruit that remains. Every one of us has impure motives that need to be dealt with. Sin is deceitful and will creep in and tempt every one of us; *even in our motive behind serving the Lord.* This is where everyone must decide to approach the Presence of God and lay aside every sinful tendency that once ruled over our lives.

What Christ accomplished on the Cross has given us access into the fire of His Presence which works in us to change us from the inside out, from glory to glory. The Bible calls this process "sanctification" which defined is "the process in which we are made holy". This process cannot be avoided but, in fact, it must be embraced. Contrary to popular teaching in today's churches, the Bible still says, *"Without holiness no man shall see God" (Hebrews 12:14).* The fire of His holiness has brought judgment upon all sin, yet His fiery love for us has reached into hell itself and snatched us from the grips of the evil one. We must make the choice to walk into the fire of His Presence and burn!

Everything changes in the Presence of God. All of our preconceived notions and ideas fall away as we are consumed with burning flames that are seven times hotter than this world has ever seen. It is in His fire where we attain a burning love for Him that is stronger than even death, hell, and the grave! Will you approach the All Consuming Fire? Will you let His fire reveal every impure motive and consume you until all that is left is burning love for Him? Let me now share with you how I have been burned in His fire.

ENCOUNTERS WITH THE FIRE

I remember as I began Bible college in 2008. My sincere desire was to attain an education, which would qualify me to receive my credentials to become a pastor. As what happens to most when they get touched by the Living God, I was "on fire" for God with an insatiable desire to share the burning in my heart. As I continued my education (yet never laying aside my pursuit of His face), everything began changing in my life. The Lord began wrecking everything that I thought I knew about Him. The fire inside me began to burn hotter and hotter as I began to apply a true biblical foundation to an already burning heart. It is very important that we get this; *fire must have something to burn!* If we do not add kindling to the fire it will burn out. The only thing which can fuel the fire of God is the Word of truth. If we do not add diligent Bible study to our burning hearts, the fire will eventually burn itself out! These two cannot exist without each other. This perfect union is what made Pentecost possible. One hundred and twenty disciples who had just spent three and a half years in the Presence of the Living Word of God produced just the right ground for fire to fall from heaven and ignite a global firestorm!

As I embarked on the journey of obedience to the voice of God and attended Bible college, I truly began to get "tried by fire." His Presence began to reveal motives in my heart and opened up the deep hidden places in my soul. The Holy Spirit revealed to me that deep down inside I was forfeiting my burning passion to only see His face for status and position amongst men. These were His exact words to me, "You arc losing the heart that burns only for me in your pursuit of a position of influence in the church and with man. You need to kill the desire inside that wants to be known amongst your peers if you ever want to be effective for My kingdom."

When the Lord revealed this to me I trembled before Him. I knew it was God speaking to me, and I knew it was the truth! I stood before the Lord, completely naked and ashamed. During this season I would hear the Lord gently whisper to me in my prayer times "selfish ambitions." Oh how I would weep because I knew He was telling me what was inside my heart.

I finally came to a completely broken place where I just simply confessed that the Lord was right and I desperately needed His help. I knew, in spite of many tears, I could not remove this thing myself. Only His grace had the power to remove this inward sinful desire. I truly believe that it was this inner cry of repentance that opened the door for God to bring His holy fire into my life.

The holiness of God demands change from us in the inward parts. Without an inward change of nature, all the outward attempts of right living will only lead us directly back into the same sinful patterns that had us bound. It is the Holy Spirit's job to bring conviction of sin (see John 16:8). When true conviction of sin enters our hearts, the only right thing to do is confess. We must understand this about the nature of God: his holiness will bring correction to us regarding anything that offends His Holy Spirit. Yet His correction is not to quench our fiery passion for Him, for He desires that we might be partakers of His holiness (see Hebrews 12:5-13). Unfortunately, if we are not guarding our hearts, God's correction can often leave us feeling discouraged. When God revealed this deep character issue in my life, the first thing my flesh did was look at the impossibility of changing myself, then I became offended at God. That "old man" wanted to rise up and complain and the voice of condemnation began whispering lies into my ears saying, "Well it doesn't matter how hard I try, I just can't do anything right. You will never be good enough for God. You might as well give up and go back into the world." Does this sound familiar to anyone?

One important thing I have learned about God is that He will never lower His standard in order to accommodate our sinful ways. Yet, I have also learned that when we humble ourselves and step out in faith and obedience, His grace will come with His power to lift us up to Him to meet His holy standard! *My grace is sufficient for you, for my power is made perfect in weakness" (2 Corinthians 12:9).* Being saved by grace does not mean that we now have an excuse to live unholy lives, but rather grace now equips us with the holy fire necessary to press toward the mark.

Now, having received this revelation from the Lord about the condition of my heart, the only thing I knew to do was dig deeper into His

Presence. Looking back, I thank God for this time. It was in this place of desperate seeking that God found in me what He was looking for all along. I was a completely broken man whose only possession was a burning heart, seeking the only One who could satisfy. This was the beginning of many mind-blowing encounters that have wrecked my life and transformed me into a desperate worshiper seeking only His face.

It was not long after this season that I had my first visual encounter with the fire of God. It was during a church service at our former home church in Elk Grove, California. A visiting speaker came that day from New Orleans (a great man of God who has since become a friend). He actually preached on "the fire of God" and of course God showed up in fire! When the Spirit of God moved powerfully through our church in a prophetic way, I was called up onto the platform. This man of God spoke into my life and started blowing on me and praying, "Fuego, fuego, fuego!" (this means "fire" in Spanish). As he was praying over me everything went red. I looked up and I saw two huge tear drop looking flames of fire in front of me. All I could feel was a literal burning piercing through my very being. I instantly fell to the ground and began crying out as loud as I could. I could not contain the burning inside which penetrated every part of me.

A few weeks after that (again at my home church), I had another powerful encounter. During the worship service the glory of God came mightily. I remember looking up and again everything was red. I watched as huge drops of fire fell from the ceiling all around the sanctuary. The fire was so intense and the burning inside was unbearable. I remember looking around the walls of our church, which are decorated with the flags of every nation. I trembled inside as I watched the flags turn, before my very eyes, into flames of fire. The fire of His Presence so engulfed me that it was as if the walls of the sanctuary were closing in on me. All I could do was scream out the name of Jesus.

The revelation hit me at this time that it was literally Jesus Himself that had just walked into the sanctuary. I looked around and everybody seemed to be completely unaware that fire was consuming our sanctuary. By this time I was wailing on the floor, crying out, "Jesus, Jesus!" I finally gained strength to look up to heaven, and there, once again, were the two giant tear drop flames gazing into me. This time I knew it was His eyes of fire. His gaze pierced into my inward being and shone light into the dark places of my heart. I can remember, even as I write this, how badly it burned, yet I cried out for more. As unbearable as it was for my flesh, my spirit cried out for more because I knew I was being freed by the Consuming Fire! I knew His fire was doing a work in me that only He could do. In those moments I received revelation from heaven that He was burning away all the sin that stood in the way of deeper intimacy with Him.

These experiences with the fire of His Presence, I believe, are the only means for complete transformation. I truly believe that in these encounters, the Lord imparts His heart and mind in the same instant that He is consuming the false ideas of who we think God is. He is giving us beauty for ashes. The Lord has burned me with a desire for Him and Him alone.

LAST THOUGHT

We need fire back in the church! I believe that in this hour God is raising up a generation of believers who will fall in love with His fiery Presence and burn for Him. A generation of worshipers who will choose to abide so close to His burning Presence that His fire will consume everything they touch. Fire has an interesting quality; *without air it will burn out!* That is why I believe it is very significant that on the day of Pentecost, the Holy Spirit came in as a rushing mighty wind *and* cloven tongues of fire that sat on every one of them. Without the wind of the Spirit the fire would have quickly gone out!

The wind of the Spirit is the most integral tool in igniting a blazing firestorm that will consume the face of the earth. Jesus said in Luke 12:49-51, *"I have come to bring fire on the earth, and how I wish it were already kindled! But I have a baptism to undergo and what constraint I am under until it is completed" (NIV).* Jesus Himself yearns to baptize us in fire. The question now is … *are you ready to burn?*

Chapter 4

WORSHIP IN THE WILDERNESS

I truly thank God for His fire; without it we would not have a driving passion for God to guide us on this journey. It has been the cry of my heart for so long to see the American church burn in the fires of revival. I long to see the church wake up from its slumber and rise to fulfill her true destiny of what we are in the earth; an "awakening" of burning passion for His Presence that would, once again, become the sole desire of His redeemed bride. The passion of my heart is to help to raise up a generation who only wants Him!

Jesus is enough! His Presence is all we need to advance His kingdom in the earth and see it prevail against the gates of hell and its dark forces. I burn inside to see a generation approach His holy fire and fall in love with the gaze of His eyes that burn with fiery love for us. I tell you the truth: *when you fall in love with the gaze of Jesus' eyes, NO OTHER LOVE WILL SATISFY!* When you have been captured by His love, that same love will naturally become the fueling fire behind everything you do in life.

In the last chapter, I shared how much we desperately need fire back in the church today. The fire of God is the means by which He will birth revival in this hour, very much like the Lord sent fire down from heaven in the days of Elijah. In that day, an entire nation had turned their backs on the God of their fathers. Yet one man, Elijah, rebuilt the altar of the Lord and stood in the face of the idolatry that had perverted his nation.

The Lord honored this man of God and answered his prayer with fire that consumed the sacrifice on the altar. At this, the entire nation fell upon their faces in the fear of the Lord, declaring Him to be their God, and they turned completely back to Him again.

One of my favorite quotes comes from the revivalist Charles Finney of Rochester, New York, which says: "If you want revival to break out in your church or in your city, just draw a circle around yourself and let fire break out right there." This has been the key to my personal walk with the Lord. I determined to stop complaining about what I think everybody else should be doing or not doing and I set my heart to burn in His Presence. As soon as I made this decision everything in my life began to change. My attitude toward God and others, my personal devotion time and many other things all took on a whole new light. Through this personal revival that took place in my life, I discovered that fire is only the beginning.

FIRE IS ONLY THE BEGINNING

"Our God is a consuming fire" (Deut. 4:24). We see this in the Exodus at Mount Sinai. God chose to reveal Himself to His people and Scripture tells us that, *"The Lord descended on it* (Mount Sinai) *in fire" (Exodus 19:18).* As the Lord descended upon the mountain, His intention was to reveal Himself to His people. This is still the intention of God's heart. Fire is only the beginning of our ongoing encounters with God. When the Lord shows up on the scene, *fire will break out;* that's just who He is—HE IS A CONSUMING FIRE. When we learn this about the Lord, then the thundering and the rumblings of His Presence will not frighten us like it did the children of Israel. God was longing to reveal Himself to His people, but they stood afar and rejected His invitation. They had seen all the wonderful works of the Lord and rejoiced in them, yet when God Himself wanted intimate relations with His people they stood at a distance. Moses, on the other hand, drew near to the Lord (see Exodus 20:18-21).

The fire of the Lord is His invitation to us to come up higher! Fire is only the beginning for those who want more of God. When the apostle John was on the Isle of Patmos, he encountered the resurrected Jesus. He heard a voice speaking from behind him that sounded like the voice of a trumpet. John turned to look and described what he beheld:

The hair on his head was white like wool ... and His eyes were like blazing fire. His feet were like bronze glowing in a furnace ... His face was like the Sun shining in all its brilliance (Revelation 1:12–16).

John goes on to describe what happened to him after he looked upon the majesty of the resurrected Lord and into His eyes of fire: *"When I saw Him, I fell at His feet as though dead" (v.17).* The Lord then goes on to deliver a message to the seven churches of Asia as John is there, beholding Him and gazing into His eyes of fire.

After this I looked, and there before me was a door standing open in heaven. And the voice I had first heard speaking to me like a trumpet said, "Come up here" (Revelation 4:1).

Fire is only the beginning, and those who are willing to burn in His fire will never be the same. In Exodus, Chapters 3 and 4, we get a great picture through Moses' first encounter with the Lord. Through these two chapters I believe we can draw a pattern for our own encounters with God.

First, we see that the angel of the Lord appeared to Moses in *"flames of fire."* Again, it seems to be a pattern in the Scriptures that oftentimes (not always) the Lord's initial manifestation amongst His people is by fire. The Lord got Moses' attention through a burning bush, yet what actually appealed to Moses was the fact that the bush was on fire but was not burned up and destroyed. I believe that this was the Lord's invitation to Moses, as it is to us all, which beckons a lost and dying world, "Come to the fire that burns with a consuming flame but will not destroy." This is just the kind of thing that would scare most people away, as this same fire scared away the children of Israel.

Scripture tells us that this fire caught Moses' attention and he turned to look at this great sight. It then says, *"When the Lord saw that he had gone over to look, God called to him from within the bush, 'Moses! Moses!'"* (*Exodus 3:4*). One important thing that we can learn about the Lord is that, when it comes to encountering His people, He is the First to initiate relationship. *Yet, it is our response to his invitation that determines the depth of intimate contact with Him! The Holy Spirit will only take each of us as far as we are willing to go.* We can only love Him because He first loved us (see 1 John 4:19). Yet we *must* draw near to Him; then He will draw near to us (see James 4:8).

We see this beautifully portrayed in the Song of Solomon. The Bridegroom is constantly pursuing His bride. He is knocking on the door while she sulks on the couch. She finally gets up to answer His beckoning and finds that her lover is no longer waiting for her, but He is leaping and skipping upon the mountaintops. The Lord has a jealous love for His bride and He is constantly beckoning us to join Him in His chambers. It is completely up to us to instantly respond if we desire intimacy in His Presence. God is so good not to reject us. Even when we reject His beckoning so often in our own business in life, He is constantly knocking on the doors of our heart.

What a picture the Scripture gives us here in Exodus. The Lord was looking upon Moses while he was busy in his work of tending sheep. When God *saw* that Moses turned aside, *then* He called out to him, *"'Moses! Moses!' And Moses said, 'Here I am'"* (*v. 4*). Again, we see God is the One who called out to Moses but it was when Moses responded to the call of God that this encounter was initiated. In other words, Moses could have very easily walked right on by and missed this opportunity to meet with the Lord.

We see a similar experience in the life of young Samuel (1 Samuel 3). Samuel, as a young boy, served under Eli the priest. When God chose to reveal Himself to young Samuel He called him by name. Not yet knowing the voice of the Lord, Samuel mistakenly went to Eli supposing he had called him. The Lord did this three times until Samuel was finally instructed by Eli to respond to the Lord by saying, "Here I am Lord, speak." This is an absolute truth about the Lord; *we must respond to Him by faith, "Without faith it is IMPOSSIBLE to please God"* (*Hebrews 11:6 emphasis mine*).

The next thing that takes place after Moses responds to the call of God and approaches the burning bush is what happens to all who respond to His call. The Lord says, *"Do not come any closer ... Take off your sandals, for the place where you are standing is holy ground" (v. 5).* The fire of the Lord is a holy Fire, and as I have stated before; the holiness of God demands change! It was the mercy of God that demanded Moses not to step any closer, lest His holiness break forth upon him and bring judgment upon his sin. It is in this place where we must take off the old walk of life, put aside the old ways, and surrender to the work of the Cross within us to be made like the One who has captured our attention. Sadly, it is in this place where many fall away. Few believers surrender to the process we all must walk through called "sanctification," which is the process of being made holy.

Those who lay down their old lives will see what happens next with Moses: *"Then He said, 'I am the God of your father, the God of Abraham, the God of Isaac, and the God of Jacob" (v. 6).* This is the place of revelation, the unveiling of the God who covers Himself with fire! *"The secret of the Lord is for those who fear Him, and He will make them know His covenant" (Psalm 25:14 NASB).* For those who approach the fire of His holiness and draw even closer in the fear of the Lord, God reveals Himself through covenant. Very much like the intimacy that is shared between a husband and a wife through the covenant of marriage, the Lord reserves the intimate secrets of His heart for those who will come into marriage covenant with Him—those who will not share their hearts with other lovers! Unfortunately, in the American church I believe we have lost the fear of the Lord and the sacredness of the marriage covenant. When the divorce rate in the church nearly exceeds the rate of the world, I believe it reflects our lack of reverence for our covenant with God.

It is in the place of revelation that true worship is expressed, *"Moses hid his face, because he was afraid to look at God" (v. 6).* Moses' only response to the revelation of God was worship (hiding his face; bowing before the Lord). When we come into this place of communion with the Almighty God, He will then begin to unveil His beauty to His children. Unfortunately, many never go on to know the Lord intimately in the place of revelation. The reason being that, in the sanctification stage, God asks us to "take off our shoes."

Many attempt to serve God as under the Law and legalism, which address only what they can and cannot do. They never get past the Law and into relationship. The devil is a liar, and his scheme is to attempt to make God look like He is withholding good things from us. Everything that God does is good! Even in separating us from the world, His heart is to bring us to Himself. He removes the death that this world brings *AND GIVES US HIS LIFE—ETERNAL LIFE!* Come on everybody! So many get caught focusing on what God has taken from them (sin, death, worldly pleasures), that they never come to the place of revelation where they realize that all they left behind only kept them from gazing at the Lord! In His goodness, He has made a way for each one of us to approach His holiness and not perish in our sins. This is the Gospel! THANK YOU JESUS!

Fire is only the beginning for those who dare to walk into the fire and surrender to the purifying process that His holy flames bring. It is in this place of revelation that we get to know the intimate secrets of God in covenant relationship. Israel knew God from a distance and Scripture tells us in Exodus 24:17, "*To the Israelites the glory of the Lord looked like a consuming fire on top of the mountain.*" Moses, on the other hand, walked into the cloud of fire and for forty days was caught up in the holy mountain and was able to be sustained without food or water as the Lord showed him the heavenly blueprints of His tabernacle that was to be built. It was this tabernacle in which God Himself would have a resting place amongst the children of Israel throughout the old covenant. Yet, upon looking at this tabernacle with prophetic eyes, Moses saw the true tabernacle of God, which was the very person of Jesus Christ! He was the One whom God sent to "*tabernacle amongst men*" (see John 1:14).

Jesus became the fulfillment of every article inside the tabernacle. From the outer courts to the Holy of Holies; Jesus is the way, the truth and the life. He *is* the ark of the covenant and the mercy seat; He *is* the shekinah glory that appeared above the mercy seat; the express image of the Father in all His glory; He *is* the showbread or the Bread of Life; He *is* the lamp stand or the Light of the world. I could go on and on about the various articles within the tabernacle of Moses, all of which were a prophetic picture of the incarnation of the God-Man Jesus Christ! All of this Moses saw as he dwelt in the midst of the fire.

Another amazing example to confirm what we can see as we dwell in the midst of the fire would be the three Hebrew boys in the book of Daniel; Hananiah, Mishael, and Azariah. These Hebrew boys made a valiant choice and refused to worship the idols of their day. Nebuchadnezzar, king of Babylon, built a huge image of himself in the days of Israel's captivity. He commanded that all who were in Babylon had to bow before this idol every time they heard the sound of instruments. Failure to obey this decree would result in the rebels being thrown into a fiery furnace— sounds a lot like the spirit of the world today. The music that is coming forth from the culture today is causing an entire generation to bow their knee to the god of this world *and they don't even realize it!*

These three Hebrew boys obeyed the Word of the Lord which specifically says in the Ten Commandments, *"Thou shalt have no other gods before me ... Thou shalt not bow down thyself to them, nor serve them: for I the Lord thy God am a jealous God" (Exodus 20:3,5 KJV)*. As a result of their obedience to the Word of God they were thrown into this fiery furnace. In fact, as they boldly declared their faith in their God before King Nebuchadnezzar, he furiously commanded that the fire be made seven times hotter to hasten the agony of the so-called rebels. Hear what Scripture says as they were tossed into the blazing furnace,

> *Then King Nebuchadnezzar was astonished; and he rose in haste and spoke, saying to his counselors "Did we not cast three men bound into the midst of the fire?" They answered and said to the king, "True, O king." "Look!" he answered, "I see four men loose, WALKING IN THE MIDST OF THE FIRE; and they are not hurt, and the form of the fourth IS LIKE THE SON OF GOD"* (Daniel 3:24-25 NKJV).

Utterly amazing! In the midst of the fire, there appeared Jesus, who is the Son of God, to the Hebrew boys and He walked around with them in the furnace. Amazingly, this was somewhere around five hundred fifty to five hundred seventy-five years before Jesus was ever born of the virgin here on the earth. Just as Moses caught a glimpse of Jesus in a prophetic sense in the fire on the mountaintop, these three Hebrew boys walked with Jesus in the midst of the fire—*Fire is only the beginning!*

Fire is the tool of purification that God uses to burn away all the sin and impurities in our lives, which can taint our perception of God. Notice that in the example of the three Hebrew boys the only thing that burned up was the ties that bound them as they were thrown into the fire. This gave them freedom to walk and talk with Jesus!

True worship only results from the revelation of the True God. If sin is left un-repented in the life of a believer then all that they believe about God can be sin-tainted and actually breed deception. This is a hard truth to swallow, but it is truth nonetheless. James 1:22 says, *"Do not merely listen to the word, and so deceive yourselves. Do what it says."* I say this only to those to whom the Holy Spirit has clearly spoken to through conviction. If sin is left unchecked within any individual to whom the Holy Spirit has personally dealt with to repent, then Scripture declares *"The sting of death is sin, and the strength of sin is the law" (1 Corinthians 15:56 NKJV).* In other words, when the Spirit of God brings conviction (the sting) of sin upon a person's heart, He also gives that individual the grace of God to overcome the sin. God does not leave us without hope, *"Where sin abounded, grace abounded much more" (Romans 5:20 NKJV).* The power of God's grace is always greater than the power of the sinful nature in the life of any born again individual. However, many reject the grace of God and refuse to repent. It is in this moment of rejection that sin will actually strengthen itself within the law that was sent to bring freedom. I have seen this multiple times in my own life when I refuse to hear the still small voice of God and deliberately disobey His prompting. The sin actually strengthens itself and becomes more difficult to become free from.

Stepping into the fire is only the beginning. As we surrender our lives to the work of the Cross, the Lord will continue to reveal Himself to us through His word. The Word of the Lord is a light that will shine into the darkness within our own hearts. If we let Him, the Word of the Lord will go to the very core of who we are and change us from the inside out.

Every single person, starting at salvation, must have their mind renewed daily. This renewal gives the Holy Spirit access to reveal Jesus to us and thus we take on the mind of Christ. As I shared in an earlier chapter, many sincere people worship a God that they do not know. All of us must come to the end of ourselves and surrender to the truth that we do not know God as He is. *"God resists the proud, but gives grace to the humble" (James 4:6 NKJV).* It is when we lay our pride on the altars and humble ourselves before Him that He truly has us where He wants us. It is in this place of brokenness before a loving God that His mercy and grace comes and lifts us into His loving arms.

I AM SENDING YOU TO PHARAOH

Let us now continue on with Moses' first encounter with the Lord. As we have seen, the angel of God appeared to Moses in a flame of fire within the bush. As Moses draws near to behold this wonderful sight, the Lord calls out to Moses from the bush and instructs him to remove his shoes. Moses obeyed the voice of the Lord, then God spoke to him revealing that He is indeed the God of his fathers Abraham, Isaac, and Jacob. At this point Moses hid his face from God.

Listen to what happens next,

The Lord said, "I have indeed seen the misery of my people in Egypt. I have heard them crying out because of their slave drivers, and I am concerned about their suffering. So I have come down to rescue them from the hand of the Egyptians ... So now, go. I am sending you to Pharaoh to bring my people the Israelites out of Egypt" (Exodus 3:7-8,10).

God appears to Moses for a purpose which is revealed right here. He has people who are living in slavery and *He is come to set them free to worship Him! "Let my people go so that they may worship me" (Exodus 8:1).*

His purpose has not changed. As glorious as our encounters with God can be, His purpose in this present age is to equip a people with His Spirit to go and set the captives free. As glorious as worship is before the throne and as glorious as our encounters are in His Presence, we will have all eternity to worship and behold Him. Yet in this present age we must lay hold of the urgent reality that this life is but a vapor in the scope of eternity. People are dying everyday who will end up in hell without Jesus! Those that tarry long enough in the place of worship will become gripped with the heart of the Father for a lost and dying world. If our worship does not produce within us a revelation of the love of God for those that do not know Him, then it is not true worship at all! When we come into a true realm of worship, we will wake up to the reality that this life is not about us; *it's all about Him!* Yes, we were created for worship. Before we can be anything else, we must be worshipers! Yet, the natural result of this love affair between the Lord God and His true worshipers is taking on the heartbeat of God. This is what we see in Moses' first encounter with the Lord.

From this point on we see the Lord reveal His power to Moses in an effort to assure him of His abiding Presence. On five occasions Moses argued with God, doubting that He had chosen the right man for the task of liberating the children of Israel. Five, in the Bible, represents grace and the ministry. None of us are capable, in our own strength, to even save ourselves if we wanted to, *"Who can say, 'I have kept my heart pure; I am clean and without sin'" (Proverbs 20:9).* Without the grace of God we can do nothing that will further the kingdom of heaven. His grace is His divine empowerment to accomplish His will in the earth. In the place where the law of sin and death tells us, "you can't do this," His grace meets us in our weaknesses and breathes the divine breath of God upon our efforts of faith. Thus, *"We can do all things through Christ who strengthens us" (Philippians 4:13).*

Moses was absolutely correct; he could not do what God was asking him to do in his own strength. Yet, we must understand that God does not choose those who think they can. God was not coming to Moses because of his skill or personality or any such thing. In fact, the apostle Paul addresses this in 1 Corinthians 1:26-27, 29:

Brothers and sisters, think of what you were when you were called. Not many of you were wise by human standards; not many were influential; not many were of noble birth. But God chose the foolish things of the world to shame the wise; God chose the weak things of the world to shame the strong ... So that no one may boast before Him.

God does not see how man sees; He looks at the heart (see 1 Samuel 16:7). There are so many people today in ministry who are very gifted and talented. Many of them have pushed their own weight to get where they are today. They have moved ahead of God and never allowed the Lord to forge them in the fire. They believe they are ready and have something to offer to the world through their "ministry" because of how gifted they are. The unfortunate thing is that if they do not lay aside trusting in themselves and their gift, they are completely useless for the kingdom. God does not need a single thing that we have to offer.

When Moses was forty years of age, he himself attempted to move ahead of God and take matters into his own hands. He rose up and slew an Egyptian who was beating one of his Hebrew brothers. Stephen testifies to this in Acts by saying, *"Moses thought that his own people would realize that God was using him to rescue them, but they did not" (Acts 7:25).* It was not for another forty years, when Moses was eighty years old, that God came to him. This was also forty years after living on the back side of the desert, tending sheep. We must understand this picture: Moses was a man that was raised up in Pharaoh's household. He was learned in all the wisdom of the Egyptians (see Acts 7:22). Yet in the prime of his life, at forty years of age and full of the world's knowledge, God could not use him! He rose up in his own strength, with all the knowledge he had learned in the greatest schools of Egypt and attempted to do the work of God and failed.

I will now be very bold and say that the devil is not intimidated by our titles or by the degrees that we post on our walls! I will be even bolder to say that such pride and arrogance can actually open the door for the devil to grab a hold in the life of one who is dependent on their education to fulfill the work of God. The devil only bows to the name of Jesus. He is not impressed with how much we have done, or how much we think we know; *only faith in Jesus moves the heavenly realms!*

Whatever it was that happened inside the heart of Moses over the forty-year span in the desert broke his self-dependent spirit. So much so that God had to convince him that He was sending him back into Egypt. This is not the same Moses who heroically jumped up to defend his brothers and killed a man. Likewise, as each of us yields to the work of God in our own lives, pride and self-dependence are what must die daily at the foot of the Cross.

MY OWN PERSONAL DESERT SEASON

When I was first saved at the age of nineteen, I remember my heart literally *burning* inside. I would lie on my bed and dream the dreams of heaven! For a little over a year I kept receiving visions from God of an open field with mountains on both sides of a large green valley. In this valley before me, as far as my eyes could see, was this great multitude of people pressed together. Night after night I would hear the gospel being preached to this multitude under a powerful anointing. I knew it was the word of the Lord because even as the word was coming forth, it was fresh revelation into my spirit. In this vision, it was my voice that was proclaiming the word of the Lord. During this season this even became the way that the Lord would speak to me through His Word. It was like I had front row seats in a great evangelistic crusade. The words that were coming out of my mouth were fresh from heaven and they were food for my spirit; it was awesome!

Night after night I would hear the Lord saying, *"Go ye into all the earth and preach the Gospel to every creature ... Go ye into all the earth and preach the Gospel to every creature ... Go ye into all the earth and preach the Gospel to every creature"* (see Mark 16:15).

I knew God was calling me to preach the gospel and I was ready to take over the world. I was on fire and fully convinced that this was my calling. I went out and told everyone I could find about Jesus. Everywhere I would go I would tell people that I was a preacher. Even though I had never stepped foot behind a pulpit, I was already putting myself in that place by faith.

About this time, I was asked by my pastor to move up with them to the Portland, Oregon area where they were starting a business in brick and stone masonry as part of their ministry. I was elated and gladly accepted their offer. In the pride of my heart, I perceived this as God's way of exalting me to a position of leadership that would work me into a place to preach; after all, that is what I was called to do, right? I remember the day I left my mom and dad's house at twenty-one years of age with my car packed up and all my belongings shoved in. As I drove off, my mom stood on the porch, waving goodbye. As I drove out of Sacramento heading north I was so excited that I could hardly stand it. For the majority of the twelve-hour drive, I prayed in the Spirit out loud, just dreaming of how soon it would be that God would put me into a place where I would be preaching. Little did I know that the next eight years would be the hardest years of my life; so hard in fact that even suicide would become an option that the devil would place before me before I eventually fell upon the Rock and became broken.

God will never use those who trust in their own ability! No matter how on fire I was for Jesus, He still took me into a desolate wilderness place and forged me in the fires of His Presence. The dream that God had placed in me seemed all but a fantasy from my own imagination over the next eight years of my life. At times I battled such insecurity that I even questioned my salvation. That fiery confidence that once burned within me seemed to vanish away during this time of testing.

It was this season in my life when I learned how to stay on my face before God and cry out. I kept my face in His Word and prayer for the majority of this season. The only time I felt close to God was when I was either in worship and prayer or reading His Word. All other times I was so insecure inside that I could barely even speak to people without them asking if I was alright; I was tormented by doubt and depression.

I remember when this all came to a climax. It seemed like everything that I even attempted to do in any area of my life just failed. Even when I would read the Scriptures I began feeling hopeless and defeated; so much so that I began contemplating walking away from the Lord altogether. I remember the day when I picked up the Word and began to read in John 6. When I read the story about the disciples not receiving Jesus' teaching about eating His flesh and drinking His blood, many were offended and stopped following Him. Jesus then turned to the twelve and said, *"You do not want to leave too, do you? ... Simon Peter answered Him, 'Lord, to whom shall we go? You have the words of life. We have come to believe and to know that you are the Holy One of God"* (John 6:67-69). In brokenness of spirit I cried out the same thing to the Lord, "Lord, where else can I go? I don't want to live this life without You. Please help me, Lord!" I had no passion for the things of God any more, yet I didn't want to feel this way. I knew He was the Lord, yet I still was ready to walk away with a rebellious attitude in my heart and I was sick of living with this rebellion.

As I continued reading, Jesus responds to His disciples and says, *"Have I not chosen you, the Twelve? YET ONE OF YOU IS A DEVIL!"* (v. 70 emphasis mine). When I read these words I felt as if the Lord Himself was speaking this to me, telling me that I was nothing more than a devil! I felt totally hopeless and lost. All desire to continue living just faded away. I immediately fell to my face in prayer and cried out to the Lord. While in prayer I felt such a demonic opposition against me that I finally gave up. The enemy put this image into my mind of a noose wrapped around my neck and he told me to take my own life. "God can never use you, He even *chose* Judas yet He knew that Judas was a failure. So just end your life now, just like Judas did, so you don't keep hurting His kingdom any longer. You are a waste of God's time because you are past being helped." These words flooded my mind and polluted my soul. I was ready to end it all! Yet, because of the fear of the Lord, I believed that if I died in that state I would wake up in hell with the same torment in my soul, but I would just be trapped forever in it.

The devil is a liar! It was in this moment that I got on my face before God and rebuked the devil and refused to believe his lie. I stayed on my face for five hours straight until the devil left me and I got up believing the truth of God's Word! It was in that moment that I received the revelation that Jesus saves us, yes, yet we *must believe in Him!* Our faith in Jesus is what saves us, not how great we are, not our talents, but *faith*. Only *faith* gives us access into the grace of God in which we stand (see Romans 5:1-2). I also realized that the devil even used Scripture against Jesus Himself when He was being tempted in the wilderness for forty days; it's not about who we are … but its all about who He is! My own pride and self-dependence was giving access to the devil to accuse me before the throne of God!

After that day, I began to walk in a true brokenness before the Lord that was only developed through these fiery trials. I stopped seeking to be used by God and I found a genuine contentment in just knowing and loving Him. Yes, I still battled, but I began fighting from this place of revelation that simply loving Jesus is the greatest weapon we have in this war. I didn't need to *be* anything, I already *was* loved by God, and He just wanted me to love Him back. This is the foundation of the heart of a worshiper.

As I look back, this was the greatest thing that could have ever happened to me! I very easily could have moved ahead of God and attended Bible college when I was first saved to receive credentials for ministry. I very easily could have worked my way up the ladder of so-called success in church by serving great men of God, the whole while carrying envy in my heart to eventually take their position. Yet it was in this wilderness place, on the back side of the desert for eight years, where God developed His character within me. Gifts are free, but character can only be forged in the fire! Anyone can step up and perform before the crowds with great charisma, yet very few people can stand with the character of God in the secret place of their own hearts with a clear conscience before His throne.

WHAT STANDS THE TEST OF TIME?

Gifted people are a dime a dozen, yet it is godly character that is a rare gem in the church today. When the rubber meets the road, it is not how we respond while living in the good times that defines our character, but it is our response when all hell breaks loose and the wine press of life is upon you; this is the tool that God uses to reveal what is in our hearts.

Not only so, but we also rejoice in our sufferings, because we know that suffering produces perseverance; perseverance, character; and character, hope. And hope does not put us to shame, because God has poured out into our hearts through the Holy Spirit, who has been given to us (Roman 5:3-5).

The sufferings of life define who we are—this is our *character!* Anyone can dance and shout when all is well and things are glorious, but very few will be found faithful in the trials to still give glory to God. Only those who love Him with all their heart, soul, mind, and strength will give Him praise in these times.

God is after building His character in our lives, not building our ministries! The character of God produces the fruit of the Spirit (see Galatians 5:22-23). Jesus said in John 15:8, *"By this My Father is glorified, THAT YOU BEAR MUCH FRUIT; so will you be My disciples"* (NKJV emphasis mine). God is not concerned about our ministries if they are not producing the fruit of the Spirit that will stand the test of time. Success in the kingdom is not measured by the numbers that attend our meetings, or even how many people get slain in the spirit at the altars. Our God is glorified when sons and daughters are raised up in His character and image to fight the good fight of faith in the face of darkness!

God did not save us from our sins so that we could become great apostles or prophets. Jesus did not die on the Cross so that we could become awesome pastors or evangelists. Let none of us fall under the assumption that the "high call" of God is to be powerfully anointed ministers of the gospel. No, our high call is to know Him and the power of His resurrection (see Philippians 3:7-14). Our life as a worshiper is our first and foremost call and everything we do "for" God should flow from the place of worship and relationship with God and one another. This love relationship with God and with others is what prophesies to the world that we are disciples of Jesus! It is not how successful we are in our ministries, or the size of our mega-churches. It's all about the love that flows out of our relationship with God and others.

I often share with the spiritual sons and daughters that God has called me to raise that it is not so important "what" we do for God that matters but "how" we do it. I truly believe that when we leave this earth we will not be judged for how much we did for God. In fact, I believe that everything we did for God will be the crowns that we cast before the throne. Nothing that we accomplish is because of our own strength or ability, only because of Jesus can we do anything. These "crowns" of accomplishment will be thrown at His feet on that day and I believe that we will be judged according to our character. In other words, *who were you in the secret place?* When the cameras are off and no one is looking, who are you in that place? God sees all things and Scripture tells us that, *"What is done in secret shall be revealed openly" (see Luke 8:17).* Our God is not so concerned about what we *do* as much as He is concerned about *who we are*! The gifts that are upon our lives are to build up His body so that we will be more like Jesus!

Godly character is what will stand the test of time! Everything that we walk through in life is to build His character within us that we might become more Christ like in all our ways. Even the gifts that God bestows upon us are to build up the body of Christ to become more like Him on the earth.

Moses caught this revelation when He stood before God. All the knowledge and wisdom of Egypt meant nothing in the Presence of Almighty God. What happened to Moses over the forty-year period in-between fleeing Egypt and meeting God at the burning bush crushed his confidence in himself. Yet what is crushed by God in our flesh, He always replaces by His character in our spirit that He will never crush again. When God called Moses at the burning bush, He came to a man who was truly ready for the work of God, *to bring an entire generation out of the same bondage that once held him captive!*

The entire congregation of Israel crumbled time after time under the pressures of the wilderness trials. For forty years all Israel, including Moses, walked through times of great and awesome miracles and they also walked through times of great suffering. Yet when the going got tough, Moses had a foundation built in the Presence of God that proved to stand in the trials when the rest of Israel crumbled. All the miracles that

God performed did not produce within the host of Israel the character to endure the trials of life; the same is true for us today. Everything that God can do *for* us, no matter how miraculous it is, will not stand the test of time when we stand before Him; *only His character contains life … only the fruit of the Spirit bears fruit that will remain in eternity!*

THE TRUE OBJECT OF WORSHIP

As we have gone through these past two chapters about the true object of our worship, I pray that you have caught an perspective of the One we call our God. If we do not have a proper image of the God we serve, then everything we do in life will be steered in the wrong direction. If we do not live in the scope of eternity, then we will not yield to God as He works within us to build the character we need to become more like Him in all we do. We must hear His heart and be taught His ways in order to endure till the end.

As we get a clearer image of the true object of our worship, then we will get a clearer vision of our purpose as worshipers on the earth. God is building up an end time army of worshipers to be His warriors in this hour. Though we will have all eternity to worship God, it is from this place of worship on the earth that we will begin to release a fragrance of His Presence that will soon cover the earth with His glory as the waters cover the sea (see Habakkuk 2:14). Let the worshipers arise and release this fragrance!

Chapter 5

SWEET SMELLING FRAGRANCE

Now thanks be to God who always leads us in triumph in Christ, and through us diffuses the fragrance of His knowledge in every place. For we are to God the fragrance of Christ (2 Corinthians 2:14-15 NKJV).

As part of the 24-7 prayer movement, I have been blessed to be in multiple gatherings where the presence of God manifests in glorious ways. It never ceases to amaze me how God can move upon many different hearts in multiple different ways. In the same meeting you can have one person lying prostrate before the Lord; another travailing and crying out at the top of their lungs; one may be completely still before the Lord with streams of tears flowing down their face, while another is dancing, spinning and laughing before the Lord.

Is there any one expression of worship that pleases God more than the other? Is there a certain "style" that pleases God more than the other? Questions like these have plagued believers and have actually been the root of churches separating for centuries. I believe the main reason this is happening is because we have made worship about us. Especially in the modern day Charismatic/Pentecostal churches. We worship until we "feel" good, completely ignorant to the truth that worship has *always* been about God!

Satan's scheme always has been and always will be to make the things of God about us. His desire is that we exalt ourselves in our own hearts and live as if God exists to please us, when in all reality we exist to worship and exalt Him in all we do. *The love of self is the root of pride and sin!* This expression of self-exaltation came from satan himself when he took his eyes off of God and looked within himself:

> *You were anointed as a guardian cherub, for so I ordained you. You were on the Holy Mountain of God; you walked among the fiery stones. You were blameless in all your ways from the day you were created till wickedness was found in you ... Your heart became PROUD on account of your beauty, and you corrupted your wisdom because of your splendor. So I threw you to the Earth; I made a spectacle of you before kings (Ezekiel 28:14-15,17 emphasis mine).*

Anytime that we make something about us, we are coming from the nature of sin (which in reality is the nature of satan). We must resist the temptation to be self-centered and learn to keep our gaze upon Jesus and yield daily to being a vessel that flows from His perfect, selfless love.

In the garden we catch our first glimpse of the devil's schemes. God gave Adam and Eve the right to "*Eat all things freely of any tree in the garden, but do not eat of the tree of the knowledge of good and evil*" *(Genesis 2:16-17)*. Yet satan was able to pervert that command just enough to take Eve's eyes off the goodness of God and His generous nature. It was then, and only then, that he was able to convince her that God was holding something good back from them, and she ate the forbidden fruit with her husband.

Adam and Eve walked in the garden of God along with all the hosts of heaven that encircle His throne day and night with worship. Because of this one act of disobedience, they lost their place before His throne and were cast out of His garden.

Keeping His throne room the center of our lives is the key to the life of a worshiper. This is the key to "fighting the good fight of faith." Everything that happens in the created universe proceeds *from* the throne room of heaven. For this reason we *must* learn to access this throne room and bring our lives before Him as a sweet fragrant offering.

INCENSE ARISING

Malachi 1:11 became a key Scripture to the Burn 24-7 movement that my wife and I are involved with. Our leader, Sean Feucht, spoke this over our Burn tribe as our mandate and mission as the 24-7 community:

My name will be great among the nations, from where the sun rises to where it sets. In every place incense and pure offerings will be brought to me, because my name will be great among the nations.

As we continually lift up our praise before God, He can't help but be attracted to the burning aroma of love coming up before His throne like incense.

Sean has had the honor of going to some of the spiritually darkest places on the earth and releasing the incense of burning love before God! As this incense rose up before His throne, others became attracted and addicted to His Presence. As a result, burn furnaces of night and day worship have kept the fires burning on the altars in these nations.

There is a fragrance that is released in the unseen realm of heaven as burning hearts, ignited by radical love for Jesus, lift up praise to the throne of Almighty God. This "fragrance" attracts the attention of the Bridegroom King. I love this Scripture in the Song of Solomon: *"While the king was at his table, my perfume spread its fragrance" (1:12).* Our Bridegroom King is attracted to the fragrance of our worship as it is coupled together with burning desire to be with Him. Psalm 22:3 even reveals that God is *"enthroned on the praises of Israel" (NLT).* In fact, at the end of the age, it is the cry of the Spirit and the lovesick bride saying, "COME!" that will compel Jesus to return for His bride. This incense of worship will become the vehicle that ushers in the millennial reign of Jesus on the earth (see Revelation 22:17).

Revelation, Chapter 8, gives an awesome account of what happens in the heavens, in the end times, when the prayers of the saints rise up like incense before the throne of God:

When He opened the seventh seal, there was silence in heaven for about half an hour. And I saw the seven angels who stand before God, and to them were given seven trumpets. Then another angel, having a golden censer, came and stood at the altar. HE WAS GIVEN MUCH INCENSE, THAT HE SHOULD OFFER IT WITH THE PRAYERS OF ALL THE SAINTS UPON THE GOLDEN ALTAR WHICH WAS BEFORE THE THRONE. AND THE SMOKE OF THE INCENSE, WITH THE PRAYERS OF THE SAINTS, ascended before God from the angel's hand. Then the angel took the censer, filled it with fire from the altar, and threw it to the earth. And there were noises, thunderings, lightnings, and an earthquake (Revelation 8:1-5 NKJV emphasis mine.)

What a glorious picture the Word of God gives us about the power of our worship and prayer as it rises before the throne of God like incense! In the throne room of heaven, where the constant sound of non-stop worship has been taking place from the beginning of creation, *God commands silence.* We must see this! God Himself silences heaven for the sole purpose to hear the prayers of His saints. The fire from the altars of heaven are coupled with our prayers on the earth, thus causing a cosmic shaking that sends thundering and lightnings into the earth. This shaking brings about His righteous end-time judgments that are the final preparations before Christ takes His rightful place as the Lord of all.

Many times in the Old Testament, God instructs the sin offerings to be offered with fire. Scripture tells us that, being coupled with fire, these offerings would come up before God as *"an aroma pleasing to the Lord" (Leviticus 1:9;2:9;3:5;6:21).* This is *awesome!* This can apply to us today as our "sacrifices of praise" (see Hebrews 13:15). Whatever flows from within us comes up before the throne of God as a fragrance; either pleasing or displeasing to God. We can come into a gathering, lift up our hands and do all the right things outwardly, but who we are deep down inside is what rises before the courts of heaven. This is the "fragrance" that God smells!

The Lord Himself brought this accusation before Israel in Isaiah 1:

"The multitude of your sacrifices—what are they to me?" says the Lord. "I have more than enough of burnt offerings ... I have no pleasure in the blood of bulls and lambs and goats ... Stop bringing meaningless offerings! Your incense is detestable to me ... I cannot bear your evil assemblies ...Take your evil deeds out of my sight! Stop doing wrong, learn to do right! Seek justice, encourage the oppressed. Defend the cause of the fatherless, plead the case of the widow" (Isaiah 1:11, 13, 16-17).

Jesus quotes another prophecy from Isaiah in Mark 7:6-8.

Isaiah was right when he prophesied about you hypocrites; as it is written: "They honor me with their lips, but their hearts are far from me. They worship me in vain; their teachings are but rules taught by men." You have let go of the commands by God in order to observe your own traditions!

It is so easy for us to fall into the trap of going through the outward motions of religion. We can pick up our Bibles and read them, yet our mind is already planning out the day ahead. We can go into the posture of prayer and even spend an hour on our faces, but never even connect with God before His throne. We do not want to lose our burning hearts that are ignited with His fiery love. *This is the danger of dead religion!* Paul gives this warning to Timothy about a sign of the end times and to watch for those who are *"lovers of pleasure [themselves] more than lovers of God. Having a form of godliness but denying its power" (2 Timothy 3:4-5).* It is for this reason that I am so jealous to see the fire of God back in His people! When fire is on the altar, then incense will arise before the throne of God that *pleases* Him. It then *pleases* God to move for us on account of our worship and prayer. Unfortunately, where there is no fire, then the sacrifice on the altar will not rise up before our God to bring Him pleasure.

Not long ago I received a vision from the Lord during prayer. He showed me a large group of people inside a building. In the center of a large sanctuary was a matchstick that was flickering with a small flame. The people inside this building were dancing and shouting around the matchstick. I then looked up and I could hear the Lord shouting, "Come up here! I AM the Consuming Fire. Come up here and burn with Me!" Yet, because of all their noise, no one could hear God. God then spoke to me: "This is a picture of the church in America today. They are content to dance around a small flicker of fire when I am calling My people to draw nearer to Me where they will become consumed in My flame. Their sacrifice of praise brings no pleasure to me, *they worship to please themselves.*"

As hard a truth as this is to swallow, I know that this vision was from the Lord. Therefore, we must contend in our worship and prayer to go past the place where we just get our own pleasure from God into the place where God receives pleasure from us. We must get this! *We are not called to the secret place for self-pleasure, but for the pleasure of God!* Mature love, the perfect love that comes from God, seeks not its own pleasure but the pleasure of its lover (see 1 Corinthians 13).

So how is it that we can offer up a "pleasing sacrifice" to God? How can our lives become a sweet fragrance before the Lord? Scripture tells us that, *"Without Faith it is impossible to please God" (Hebrews 11:6).* Coming to God *by faith* is the only way to bring pleasure to His heart. It is only by faith that our offering will become a pleasing incense before the Lord.

Many worship and pray from a place of being defeated as if they need to beg God to come to their rescue. This kind of offering brings no pleasure to God! In the unseen realm of heaven, it is the prayers of the righteous, when prayed in *faith,* that tip the "bowls" and send the quaking and the shaking of His Presence into the earth. The Spirit of God does not move in response to the needs of His people; He responds to our faith. When we couple our worship and prayer with faith, then what happens in the unseen realm is moving His Spirit already on our behalf. Though we might not see it with our natural eyes, we can believe by faith that God is already releasing the answer into the earth.

Still you might be asking, "What is faith"? Faith can be the most complex component to anyone who attempts to live for God in their mind or intellect. We cannot figure God out in our minds. The Lord has always been the God who is past finding out (see Romans 11:33). Yet the simplicity of God is that man, in his own wisdom, cannot find Him; yet He reveals Himself to babes with child-like faith (see 1 Corinthians 1:27-28). This is astounding and offensive to the proud in heart who long to boast about their knowledge, but this revelation is fuel for worship to the humble in heart. *When we come before God in simple child-like faith, He sends fire upon our sacrifice of worship.*

As I stated earlier, *"The love of self is the root of pride and sin."* The nature of sin (also called "the flesh" in KJV) is always warring against the spirit within us in an attempt to remove ourselves off of the altar of God, where the "old man" dies. This is the mystery of the Cross: *That Christ died on the Cross to save us from the nature of sin, BUT WE MUST TAKE UP THAT SAME CROSS, AND DIE DAILY!* This is the truth of the gospel that has almost all but disappeared in the modern church of America. The preaching of the Cross is an offense to those who choose to live for themselves. Unfortunately, in the church today, we have taken the offense of the Cross out of much of the church at large to make way for a gospel that teaches of a God who will fellowship with our selfish, compromised lives.

The true Christian life is not that we get to say a prayer in a church building and go to heaven when we die. In fact, this is becoming one of the great deceptions that is perverting the Gospel in this hour. Too many are just saying a sinner's prayer at an altar and leaving the house of God the same way they came in. There is no desire or conviction that their lives must change from that day forward. NO! The true Christian life reflects the "good news" that we are no longer bound to live in this depraved state outside of the Presence of God. The Gospel is not that we get to go to heaven when we die, but that we bring heaven into the Earth through our surrendered lives! We are already dead in Christ, but made alive by His Spirit!

If we come to these altars and *stay on these altars,* then the power of the blood of Jesus equips us to live filled with the same Spirit that raised Jesus from the dead. By "picking up the Cross" we live our lives as a living sacrifice on the altars of God in heaven. We then "die daily" and become the fragrance of Christ on the earth. THIS IS THE GOSPEL! We now live for God and not for ourselves any longer, in having to obey the lusts that once drove us away from the Presence of God. The Scripture even declares that God works death in us so that His life can become known to others (see 2 Corinthians 4:12; Philippians 3:10). To the selfish world our sacrifice is an offensive smell of death, but before the throne of Almighty God it is the smell of life!

Again, *"Without faith it is impossible to please God."* So what is "faith"? Hebrews 11:1 tells us *"Faith is the substance of things hoped for, the evidence of things not seen" (NKJV).* The New Testament word for "faith" in the original Greek language is "pistis" which is "persuasion and conviction especially showing a reliance on Christ for salvation and a constancy of such profession."[1] In other words, faith is more than just "believing" or a "mental assent" into Christianity. It is a living force when applied to Christ that produces *obedient living.* Many times when the words "believed or belief" were mentioned in the New Testament, there was a direct correlation with obedience. True Christian faith is always coupled with obedient living! That is why James could say, *"Faith without works is dead" (James 2:26).*

Obedience is the pleasing aroma that comes up before the throne. We cannot obey without faith! There is nothing complicated about faith, but when we attempt to live for God our own way we will not please Him by faith. The Scripture tells that, *"Faith cometh by hearing, and hearing by the word of God" (Romans 10:17 KJV).* In other words, when God speaks, our faith responds to God and is seen through our obedience to what God has spoken. *Thus God receives pleasure in our obedience.* It really is that simple. The simplicity of the gospel is that by faith we have access to the grace of God that empowers us to live obedient lives. Through our obedient, laid-down lives we become an offering and a sweet fragrance throughout the earth.

When we simply obey the gospel and give our lives to Jesus, we receive the promised Holy Spirit, which will guide us into all truth. Yes, we will war against the nature of sin within us because our flesh has only desire to please "self" and not God. But, as we continue to lie on our faces before God, His fire will consume us on the altars. Our God is a consuming fire and when we lie before Him with a desperate heart, His fire will devour everything within us that hinders His love from consuming us.

If we do not yield to the process of dying daily, then we will only see and feel the pain of death and complain about the suffering. But when our eyes are kept on the prize, who is Jesus Himself, then we partake of the night and day worship that continues before His throne. We will then walk in the revelation that, *"The sufferings of this present time are not worthy to be compared with the glory that shall be revealed"* (Romans 8:18 NKJV). One of the greatest fights that the devil throws before us is to tempt us to look upon our own selves and complain about the suffering of the Cross. Life will always have its ups and downs. This is why I believe that worship is an absolute key to our walk with God. When we give ourselves to the altars of God and worship Him, then in the same moment that our trials are killing the old man, our spirits are ravished by His pleasure and we are not swallowed up in the pain of death.

By faith, we escape the pains of death and access the realm of life. By faith, we are convinced that God is far above able to fulfill His will as we embrace the Cross. By faith, we give ourselves over to death so that His life can be manifested through us. It is by faith that we access the pleasure of the heart of God as we become obedient unto death just as Jesus Himself became obedient to death on the Cross. Thus the world will see the beauty of Jesus through our obedience. *This is the fragrant incense that arises to bring pleasure to our God and Father!*

THE SECRET PLACE

Faith and obedience are what bring pleasure to God. I will now bring this all around and say that it pleases God most when we are simply ourselves before Him. We don't have to pretend or perform for Him or others. If we are weak in our faith, we don't have to pretend to be strong. God knows who we are. He knows where we are at, and He loves us nonetheless.

Before we were ever in our mother's womb, God formed us and called us by name (see Jeremiah 1:5). He knows who we are because He created us!

For you created my inmost being; you knit me together in my mother's womb. I praise you because I am fearfully and wonderfully made; your works are wonderful, I know that full well. My frame was not hidden from you when I was made in the SECRET PLACE. When I was woven together in the depths of the earth (Psalm 139:13-15 emphasis mine).

The fragrance of our worship before the Lord proceeds from the secret place within us. This is the place where many of us can hide from others, but it is completely open to the Lord. The Father Himself *dwells* in this secret place, and we too must come to Him in the "secret place."

During His Sermon on the Mount, Jesus made a profound statement while teaching His disciples about giving, praying, and fasting. He starts off by saying, *"Be careful not to practice your 'acts of righteousness' before men to be seen of them. If you do, you will have no reward from your Father in heaven" (Matthew 6:1).* Instead, Jesus then reveals to them, three separate times, to give, pray, and to fast to *"your Father who sees what is done in secret, will reward you"* (see Matthew 6:4,6,18).

What Jesus is telling His disciples, *in the midst of multitudes,* is mind blowing. Again in Luke 12:1-3 it says,

In the meantime, when an innumerable multitude of people had gathered together, so that they trampled one another, He began to say to His disciples first of all, "Beware of the leaven of the Pharisees, which is hypocrisy. For there is nothing covered that will not be revealed, nor hidden that will not be known. Therefore whatever you have spoken in the dark will be heard in the light, and what you have spoken in the ear in the inner rooms will be proclaimed on the housetops (NKJV).

SWEET SMELLING FRAGRANCE

What we do in the secret place speaks louder than what we do in public places! We cannot get caught up in performing before men, but instead we must live for the Lord Himself, who abides in what Jesus refers to as the "secret place."

It is innate within the soul of man to seek the approval of another. In fact, this "seeking" was placed there by the Lord Himself and can only be perfectly satisfied with the attention of God. Within the core of our soul is a longing to love and to be loved. In the "secret place" of our hearts, the very inner chambers of our soul, is where God Himself desires to awaken our spirits, lavish His love upon us, and to even dwell within us. Because of the nature of sin that has ruled over man without Christ, many unknowingly strive for approval of others rather than our Father in heaven. In the secret places of the heart our motives are often driven by everything *but* the perfect love that proceeds from God. Therefore we must place an emphasis in our own lives on the importance of establishing a secret place with the Father. The Lord does not see as man sees; He looks into the heart or "the secret place."

In the Old Testament, the Lord gave specific instruction to Moses and the children of Israel on how to build His tabernacle in which God Himself would dwell with Israel during their journeys for forty years in the wilderness. God was very specific in His instruction and called by name the men who were to build this tabernacle. Within the structure of the tabernacle there were three distinct parts: The outer court, the inner court (also called the holy place) and the most holy place (or Holy of Holies).

The outer court was the place where people would bring their sin offerings. The priests would then kill the offering on the brazen (brass) altar and wash themselves at the brazen laver before entering the inner court.

Within the inner courts, only the priests were permitted to enter. This was the place where the altar of incense, the table of the showbread (or the bread of the Presence), and the golden lamp stand were placed. All three of these articles in the inner court are representations of the person of Jesus Christ. The incense represents the prayers of the saints that rise up before the throne and also represents Christ as the One who ever lives to make intercession for us (see Hebrews 7:25). The golden lamp stand represents Christ who declared Himself to be the "Light of the World" (see John 7:12). Finally, the showbread (or bread of the Presence) represents Christ as the Bread of heaven (see John 6:35).

Now we come into the Holy of Holies, which was separated from the inner court by a thick veil. Within the Holy of Holies was placed the ark of the covenant. This place was completely off limits except to the High Priest, who was only allowed to enter once a year on the Day of Atonement, and not without blood to cover his own sins and the sins of the nation. Upon the cover of the ark was what was called the mercy seat that rested between the two cherubim of glory. It was here, between the cherubim, and above the mercy seat, that God promised to meet with Moses and the future high priests (see Exodus 25:22).

The Holy of Holies was the place where the undiluted Presence of God dwelt; within the veil and completely off limits to any man other than the high priest during the period of the Old Testament. So Holy was this place that if the high priest came before the Presence of God in an unworthy manner, he would drop dead on the spot.

When Jesus died upon the Cross, Scripture tells us that this veil that separated the inner court from the most holy place was torn from top to bottom (see Matthew 27:51). Being torn from top to bottom signified that God Himself was the One who tore down the veil that separated humanity from His undiluted, holy Presence. Where man was once separated from God is now open for all to come before Him by the blood of Jesus! We can now come boldly before the throne of grace to obtain the mercy and grace for help in our time of weakness (see Hebrews 4:16). This place that was once off limits; *the place where God Himself dwells,* we now have access to come before Him!

I believe the Holy of Holies is the place that Jesus also referred to as "the secret place" where the Father Himself dwells. It represents the dwelling place of God! Our bodies are referred to by Paul in 1 Corinthians 6:19 as the *"temple of the Holy Spirit."* Just like the tabernacle built by the hands of man during the days of Moses, human beings can be described in three distinct parts: body, soul, and spirit. We ARE the temple of God

SWEET SMELLING FRAGRANCE

made without human hands, created by the Lord Himself. We are created by God to host His Presence within us. Deep in the core of our being is the resting place of God!

The secret place is the place deep within us where flesh and blood cannot go. Beyond this veil of flesh we can find the resting place of God within us. God is Spirit and those who worship Him must worship in spirit and truth. The secret place of the Most High God is His sanctuary where He defines us and shines His image through us. As I mentioned earlier, we must make it the number one priority in our lives to establish a secret place with God. No one else but God can take you there. Who we are in the secret place is what heaven sees. It is our devotion to the secret place day in and day out where God shapes us and molds us to become more like Him.

We must devote ourselves to a life of worship and prayer. In fact, in Acts 6, the Apostles were confronted with a situation where some of the church was beginning to complain about their needs not being met by the leaders. The Apostles made a decision to have godly men appointed to this service but they themselves would *"devote themselves to prayer and the ministry of the word" (Acts 6:4)*. They understood the importance of maintaining a life of worship and prayer in the secret place.

In the life and ministry of Jesus, these same men walked and talked with the Son of God. They ate and drank with Him day in and day out. They witnessed miracle upon miracle and His interaction with the people as they flocked from the four corners of Israel to chase after this man Jesus. They also witnessed the busyness and the pressures of the ministry, so much at times that they didn't even have room for themselves or time to eat (see Mark 2:2). Yet, in the midst of all the busyness, they also witnessed a man who made time for prayer. Time after time, Jesus would sneak away from the crowds to spend time with the Father. This was such a pattern in the life of Jesus that the disciples asked Him one day, *"Lord, teach us to pray" (Luke 11:1)*. They didn't ask Him how to heal the sick, how to fill houses with people, or how to feed the multitudes. *They asked Him, "TEACH US TO PRAY!"*

Whatever it was about the prayer life of Jesus and His devotion to the secret place, it gripped the Apostles with a longing to pray like He prayed. They desired to connect with the Father like He connected with His Father. Can you imagine for one moment what it would be like to hear Jesus pray? Time after time the Son of God would petition the Father with the very heart that the Father gave Him to redeem fallen man. In fact, we get a small glimpse into this glory in John 17. This entire chapter is the Son of God speaking with God His Father. This is no accident that the Lord gave us this insight in Scripture. *He wants us to catch the heartbeat of the Son crying out "Abba Father."*

The Apostles put two and two together; *everything they saw in the public ministry of the Son of God proceeded from the place of communion that He had with His Father in the secret place!* The fragrance of the kingdom of God was released into the earth because this one Man Jesus knew how to petition the courts of heaven on behalf of the heart of the Father. An incense arose from the secret place of the Son of God that pleased the heart of the Father to answer His cry and release His Presence into earth.

LET THIS BECOME OUR CRY

Let this be our cry in this hour; *that we learn to pray like Jesus prayed! That we would contend in the secret place of the Most High God for our cities and nations!* What if we really believed that what we do in the secret place where no one is watching will be rewarded by the Father in the public places where sin now reigns? Let us have the faith to believe that the fire that we tend in the secret place of the altars in heaven can become the fire of revival that burns openly on the earth!

This generation is beginning to walk in this revelation as Houses of Prayer and Burn Furnaces are opening in great numbers worldwide. A consistent fragrance is rising up before the courts of heaven as night and day worship and prayer is becoming the voice of a generation. Cities around the world are becoming open to the move of God through the night and day prayers of a faithful few who are devoting themselves to keeping the fires burning when no one else is watching.

It is the continual prayers of the faithful remnant in the earth that I

SWEET SMELLING FRAGRANCE

believe will be the vehicle that ushers in the second coming of Jesus Christ. It's the fragrance of worship coming from the heart of a lovesick bride that will ultimately persuade the Bridegroom King to no longer hold back from coming and sweeping His bride off of her feet into the everlasting kingdom of the Lord and His Christ!

Chapter 6

THE FRUIT
OF WORSHIP

I am the vine, you are the branches. He who abides in Me, and I in him, bears much fruit ... By this My Father is glorified, THAT YOU BEAR MUCH FRUIT; so you will be My disciples (John 15:5,8 NKJV emphasis mine).

We are in a great need in this generation for a genuine move of God. Church as it has been known is just not cutting it anymore. Our cultural relevance, flashy conferences, and Sunday morning services are not bringing the deliverance needed to pull a human soul from the darkness of this age into His glorious light. If this next generation does not have genuine encounters with the Living God, then I am truly afraid to imagine what America will look like five, ten. or even fifteen years down the road if the Lord chooses to tarry.

Fortunately, we do not have a God who is intimidated by the antichrist agenda that currently pushes its way into our culture. Nor is there any darkness that does not *instantly* flee when Light shows up. Our God is not surprised by the darkness of this hour. He is not sitting on His throne in heaven saying, "Oh no, what are we gonna do now?" In fact, all of the wars and rumors of wars, the false ideologies and agendas, the earthquakes and the famines are playing right into the hands of the Lord. What the devil means for destruction, our God will turn it around for His good ... HALLELUJAH!

The last hour of this age is foretold in Scripture to be the darkest hour of human history. In fact, Jesus makes a statement in Matthew 24:22 that it will be such intense suffering that He will cut that hour short for the elect's sake. Something that is misunderstood by the people of God, especially in the western world, is that *the Lord is not so concerned about our comfort in this life as much as He is set on restoring mankind back into right relationship with Him.* The primary purpose of God in this age is the restoration of what was lost in the garden due to the sin of Adam and Eve.

It is a fact that this hour will be dark. But the Word of God also prophesies that in this same hour will also be the greatest harvest of souls that the world has ever seen. It will be the greatest outpouring of the Holy Spirit that will far exceed even the book of Acts. It is the end time harvest of the precious fruit that the Father has had longsuffering for since the beginning; *this is the will of God!*

In John 15:8 Jesus makes a powerful statement that has changed my life to this day. *"By this My is Father glorified, that you bear much fruit; so you will be my disciples"* (NKJV).

When I was young in the Lord, I gave my all into doing as much as I could do for the Lord in order to please Him. In my insecurity, I fell under the trap of believing that, because I was being used by God, I was getting His stamp of approval on my life. When we first come to the Lord and receive the baptism of fire, our heart becomes inflamed with a hunger to minister and be used by God. We believe ourselves to be unstoppable because we are fueled by the heart of God to reach into hell itself and rescue all who are in the devil's grip. For most new comers to Christ, this is an awesome and memorable season of the newness of being set free and set apart to the purpose of God in their lives.

The Lord has placed within every soul gifts and talents that, when used for the kingdom, will shake cities and nations. Yet, as awesome of a truth as this is, we must learn that the Father is not glorified in our works of ministry, but in the fruit that we bear through abiding in the Vine.

GIFTS VS. FRUIT

Before I go on any further with this thought, let's examine the difference between the "gifts of the Spirit" and the "fruit of the Spirit." For some, this may not cause any confusion, but I myself have witnessed the deception that many fall into. This deception is a belief that, because they are used by God, this is His seal of the "fruit" of their maturity. Let me explain why I believe this to be a misconception.

I made a statement at the end of Chapter 4 in the section "What stands the test of time" saying, "gifts are free but character is forged in the fire." I will continue with this thought by now likening character as "fruit." The "fruit of the Spirit" is the character of God, but the "gifts of the Spirit" are the works of God. There is a difference between these two, though He is the same God.

Psalm 103:7 says, *"He [God] made known His ways to Moses, His deeds to the people of Israel."* In this Scripture we see a distinction between the works (deeds) of God and the ways of God. Though Israel saw the works of God and rejoiced over His mighty miracles that they witnessed time after time, *they never knew His ways!* Only Moses drew near to God to learn His ways because He chose to abide in His Presence. Carefully consider this thought: *God's ways can be learned through His works if our heart is set on knowing His ways, but only knowing His works will NEVER substitute for knowing His ways and abiding in His Presence.* It is only as we behold Him (not His works) that we are transformed into the same image from glory to glory (2 Corinthians 3:18).

Many young and immature believers fall into the trap of finding their identity in what they are doing for God but never can find security in who they are in Him. There is no condemnation in this statement; it is just a reality of our walk in Christ. Just as a baby falls many times while learning to walk, so will young, immature believers fall into this same trap while growing in relationship with Christ. Anyone who has accepted Christ and has been filled with His Spirit is born again—they are sons and daughters by nature. Our identity is found in who we are in Christ NOT by what we do for Him.

The Corinthian church fell into this trap. In his letters to Corinth, the apostle Paul had to immediately address issues with these new believers. Most scholars believe that the Corinthian church was somewhere around five to seven years old when these letters were written. They were a very young church that was thriving in the gifts of the Spirit. In fact, that is why Paul brought forth his teaching and revelation regarding the nine gifts of the Spirit, particularly tongues and prophecy, and orderly worship in public gatherings. Paul brought order to what was taking place in the church as the Holy Spirit was moving in powerful ways. Yet in the same letters, Paul had to confront these young believers about their open sin and disorderly conduct in the church. Though this church was being used by God to shake the city of Corinth and the region of Achaia (see Acts 18) they lacked the character or "fruit" that truly brings glory to the Father in heaven.

When we stand before the Lord, I am convinced that all of our works accomplished through our gifting and ministries will be cast before the feet of Jesus. The "crowns of righteousness" (see 2 Timothy 4:8) that we earn by running this race faithfully will be cast before His throne. But who we are in secret is what will be opened up before God. This is the "fruit" that will remain! Our works can be burned up but who we are in our character is the fruit that will speak before the courts of heaven on the Day of Judgment.

In Matthew 7:21-23, Jesus finishes His famous sermon on the mount with a gripping revelation. He says,

Not everyone who says to me "Lord, Lord," will enter the kingdom of heaven, but only the one who does the will of My Father in heaven. Many will say to me on that day, "Lord, Lord, did we not prophecy in Your name, and in Your name drive out demons and perform many miracles?" Then I will tell them plainly, "I never knew you. Away from Me, you evil doers!"

Lets first of all establish what Jesus is referring to when He says, *"On that day."* What "day" is He talking about? He is talking about the Judgment

Day as confirmed in the New Living Translation. Judgment Day is the day that Scripture foretells when the books will be opened and we will all be judged according to our "works" while living here on earth. Many believers are misguided in believing that, as a Christian, we will not stand before Jesus as a judge because we have been saved from any judgment. This is not what Scripture teaches. Paul says to the Church, not to the world, in 2 Corinthians 5:10:

> *For WE must all stand before the judgment seat of Christ that each one may receive what is due him for the things done while in the body, whether good or bad* (emphasis mine).

It is also important for us to see that this group that Jesus is addressing is calling Him "Lord, Lord" signifying that, during their lives on earth, they came to the knowledge of Jesus Christ as Lord.

This Scripture has always produced within me a genuine foundation for the holy fear of God. The New Testament Jesus that we all claim to know and love gives us a vivid picture of the judgment seat where *many*, not a few, but MANY will come to Him calling Him "Lord." This company will be coming to Him with many works of ministry done *in His name* and He will declare that He never knew them. WOW! These people believe with all their heart that they were doing the will of the Father, but will stand before Jesus in complete shock as He declares that He never knew them.

It is important to grasp, from this account, that just because we are working the works of God through our gifts and ability is not our evidence that we have intimate fellowship with God. There is an absolute distinction between doing His work *through* us and producing His fruit *in* us.

The word that Jesus uses in Matthew 7:23 for "knew" in the original Greek is "ginosko." This word carries a much deeper meaning than a simple intellectual knowledge that can be obtained through study. It literally means "to know, to come to know by experience." It signifies an ongoing, unfolding knowledge obtained through intimate relationship.1 Other uses of this word even translate to "sexual intimacy." I believe that this word can help to describe a deeper lever of true worship. True biblical worship, in its purest form, is intimacy with God that produces His nature within us. The nature of God can also be called "the fruit of the Spirit." We learn of this fruit in the book of Galatians 5:22-23, "But the fruit of the Spirit is love, joy, peace, patience, kindness, goodness, faithfulness, gentleness and self-control." The fruit of the Spirit is what is produced in us through intimate fellowship with God and is perfected in us through the fiery trials of life. On the other hand, the gifts of the Spirit are freely available to all who are filled with the Spirit and are for the edifying or building up of others. Gifts are free, but the fruit of the Spirit will cost us our own lives and will mature through time as we walk with the Lord.

Jesus was addressing a people who did many things for Him and witnessed many miracles. Much like Israel in the wilderness, *they never came to His holy mountain to intimately know His heart!* God is not interested in us doing *for* Him if it is not reflecting His character and bringing glory *to* Him. This is why I believe we have the great "Love Chapter" in 1 Corinthians 13 sandwiched between Paul's teaching on the spiritual gifts. Though this church was thriving in the gifts of the Spirit, they lacked the maturity of ministering through God's love, which produces the fruit of the Spirit. Paul had to correct them for the envy and strife that was also thriving in their midst. From the beginning of this letter, Paul deals with the Corinthians in a corrective manner.

I believe the Corinthian church becomes a picture for us today of a people who loved the "gifts" but neglected the "fruit" or character of God. I have seen this time and time again. Many people seek after being used by God. They will pursue positions of ministry or notoriety amongst peers. They race to microphones and large platforms. They believe this will fill the void inside that can only be filled by being perfectly loved by God.

Do not get me wrong, Scripture tells us to "eagerly desire spiritual gifts" but *"follow the way of love" (1 Corinthians 14:1).* God gives to each of us gifts and talents that we are required to put to use. We will even give an account for our faithfulness with these gifts. Unfortunately, what happens to many of us is that we can become "works" driven and not "love" driven. In other words, without love being the driving force behind all we do, our works profit nothing. This is what Paul is telling the Corinthian church in 1 Corinthians 13. This chapter is more than just something we read at weddings. Paul is addressing a young church that was missing the whole purpose of what God was doing in their midst. He says to them that they can *"speak in the tongues of angels ... have the gift of prophecy, fathom all mysteries and have all knowledge ... and have faith to move mountains, and even give your bodies to be burned ... yet without love it profits nothing."*

Sadly, this generation is being called "The Fatherless Generation." This fatherless generation is full of people with an orphaned spirit. These spiritual orphans have never come to the intimate knowledge that their Father loves them. What happens in the life of one with an orphaned spirit is that they will "do, do, do" in order to earn their Father's love but will never produce the fruit of a true son or daughter. A true son or daughter does everything from the place of knowing they are loved. It is in this place of the intimate love of God that the fruit of worship grows into maturity.

Worship *is* spiritual intimacy. Without intimacy there is no seed that is transferred. Where there is no seed transferred, there can be no fruit, and where there is no fruit, the Father is not glorified.

Jesus says in John 12:23-24,

The hour is come, that the Son of man should be glorified. Verily, verily, I say unto you, except a corn of wheat [seed] fall into the ground and die, it abideth alone: but if it die, it bringeth forth much fruit (KJV emphasis mine).

Jesus made this statement referring to Himself. *He is the Seed of heaven!* Jesus was referring to His death on the Cross and His life being the seed sown into the ground to die in order to bring forth the fruit of many sons and daughters into the kingdom. This is how the Father was glorified! There is also a principle that we can learn from Jesus' words which is this: *Unless we pick up the same cross and follow Jesus to His death, we are just doing religious works. But if we die with Him, we will also encounter the resurrection power that bears forth fruit to our Father.*

Being used in the gifts of the Spirit costs us nothing. In fact, God can use a donkey if He chooses (see Numbers 22-25), BUT THE LORD IS AFTER FRUIT! Bearing fruit will cost us everything. It will cost us our lives. Jesus continues immediately in John 12 to say,

> *The man who loves his life will lose it, while the man who hates his life in this world will keep it for life. Whoever serves Me must follow Me [into His death AMP]; and where I am, My servant also will be. My Father will honor the one who serves Me* (vv. 25-26).

The Lord spoke this to me recently as I heard my wife ministering to a dear sister. He said, *"I only resurrect dead things. If you still hold on to the last bit of your own life that I have sentenced to death then you will never see My resurrection power."* He then opened up the Scripture to me in 2 Timothy 3:4-5 that says in the last days many will be *"...lovers of pleasure [themselves] more than lovers of God, having a form of godliness but denying its power."*

Those who love their own lives more than they love God are afraid to "die" with Him. They might do many things "in His name" like those in Matthew 7, but it is for their own pleasure. Much like the Corinthian church, they will operate in the gifts of the Spirit. Signs, wonders, and miracles will even follow them. Yet, because they have not died to themselves, their only motivation is their personal agenda and selfish ambition, not love for God. They never produce the fruit of the Spirit in their character because they have never embraced the Cross. These are in danger of standing before Jesus on that day and being forever cast away from His Presence.

The good news is that we are not of this company if we are radical lovers of Jesus! The ones who have given themselves fully to His glorious Presence to die daily to their own agenda are the ones who will encounter the resurrection power of Christ! Not only in works of ministry but also in the revelation of His beauty during times of intimacy with the Lord Himself. Worship is intimacy! Those who die with Jesus will also be resurrected with Him and experience worship and intimacy with God that is reserved for those who hold nothing back from Him. HALLELUJAH!

THE WORD BECOMES FLESH

In everything that God does on the earth through the ministry and gifts of the Holy Spirit within His people there is purpose. Every gift, every talent, every church, and every ministry has one purpose. That purpose is to testify about Jesus. Scripture tells us in Revelation 19:10, *"the testimony of Jesus Christ is the spirit of prophecy."* When we have the mature fruit of the Spirit in our lives then everything we do for God is motivated by love for God *and* His people. Our witness of Jesus will not be tainted by the love of self. By this, true prophetic ministry is in operation through perfect love.

The Father did not send His Son into the world to die on the Cross so that we could become famous apostles and prophets. Jesus did not give His life so that we could have an international ministry or be pastors of mega-churches.

> *Therefore, when Christ came into the world, He said: "Sacrifice and offering you did not desire, but a body you have prepared for me; with burnt offerings and sin offerings you were not pleased. Then said I 'Here I am—it is written about me in the scroll—I have come to do Your will, O God"* (Hebrews 10:5-7).

Christ did not come into the world so that we could do a lot of ministry stuff for Him (sacrifices and offerings). His desire is to dwell in us (*"But a body you have prepared for Me"*). It has been God's will since the beginning, in the garden of Eden, to dwell in our midst. He desires to find a resting place on the earth within the hearts of His sons and daughters.

In Genesis 3:15, God decreed over the serpent (satan) *"I will put enmity between you and the woman, and between your seed and her Seed; He shall bruise your head, and you shall bruise His heel" (NKJV).* It is my belief that this verse is the turning point in Scripture as it prophetically declares what Christ accomplished at the Cross some four thousand years later. The "seed" of the woman became a Man that crushed the authority (head) of satan. This authority or headship was handed to satan by Adam through his one act of disobedience. Following Genesis 3:15, the whole Old Testament is the unfolding of God's plan to bring the "seed" of the woman into the earth who was destined to take back what was forfeited by Adam in the garden.

Adam and Eve were created by God to be His son and daughter that would carry within them the seed of heaven. We can also refer to this seed as the DNA of God. Also within them was the "breath of life" which can just as easily be translated as "the Spirit of God."[2] Unfortunately, through one act of disobedience the Spirit departed and the seed was tainted and corrupted (though the Seed of heaven will always remain incorruptible). From this time, the Holy Spirit would visit throughout history and rest upon different judges, kings and prophets foretelling the plan of God through their prophetic acts and the writings of the prophets.

The ministry of the Holy Spirit *always* points to Jesus. The inspired (or "in-Spirited") Scriptures of the prophets constantly pointed to the fulfillment of the "seed" becoming a Man that Israel would call their Messiah. Even the inspired acts recorded in the historical books of the Bible (Joshua-Esther) are types and shadows of what Christ accomplished through His life, death, and resurrection.

Again, what I am trying to point out here is the purpose of the "gifts" through the ministry of the Holy Spirit. They will forever point us to the revelation of Jesus Christ.

I understand that right now many of you might be saying, "Yes, Yes, of course everything in the Bible points to Jesus. I already know that!" My question to you is: Do you really know? Do you really understand, by revelation, who Jesus is? In Matthew 16:13-20 Jesus turned to His disciples and asked them one of the most important questions in the Bible. He asked them, *"Who do people say the Son of Man is?"* Now at this point His disciples did a very good job of echoing what others were saying. *"Some say John the Baptist; others say Elijah; and still others, Jeremiah or one of the prophets."* We, too, can often do a fine job of echoing what others tell us about Jesus. We can quote what Mom and Dad told us through the years or what Pastor so and so preaches every Sunday. We can even passionately testify to others about what God has done for other people.

What Jesus asks them next is the question of a lifetime for every worshiper. *"'But what about you?' He asked. 'Who do YOU say I am?"*

THE FRUIT OF WORSHIP

(emphasis mine). This is the question of a lifetime for us because true worship is only produced when we answer this question correctly. WHO DO YOU SAY JESUS IS! Not others, not Pastor so and so, but you! *"Simon Peter answered, 'You are the Christ, the Son of the Living God.' Jesus replied, 'Blessed are you, Simon son of Jonah, for this was not revealed to you by man, but by My Father in heaven.'"*

The Revelation of Jesus Christ is the only fuel for true worship! Simon Peter's response did not come from what others were saying, but straight from the personal revelation that came from the Father and the Holy Spirit. The same is true for us today. Without the revelation of Jesus there is no "fruit" in our worship. The ministry of the Holy Spirit is to reveal Jesus. It is only when we rightly see Jesus that true worship will proceed from us to the heavenly Father. True revelation produces mature fruit in our worship.

So again, who is this Jesus? I believe the greatest verse that unveils this mystery is found in John 1. *"In the beginning was the Word, and the Word was with God, and the Word was God. He was with God in the beginning"* *(John 1:1-2)*. John then continues in this beautiful unfolding of the God-Man Jesus Christ by revealing:

The Word became flesh and made His dwelling among us. We have seen His glory, the glory of the one and only Son, who came from the Father, full of grace and truth (v. 14).

I LOVE THIS! Jesus Christ is the Word of God. He proceeded from the Father in the beginning. When God spoke in Genesis 1:3, *"Let there be light,"* *we see Jesus!* Jesus is the Word that proceeded from the Father's mouth. We see Jesus in the beginning with God the Father as the spoken Word that proceeded out of the Father's mouth. This Word is the Light in the world that shone into the darkness, and that Light is Jesus Christ! We also see the Holy Spirit hovering over the waters and following after Jesus (the Word) and partnering with Him in bringing the will of the Father to pass.

What a beautiful revelation of the Son of God within the Trinity. We see the Godhead working together in perfect unison to bring forth the creation. Jesus is so much more than a man that we see painted in pictures with a beard, sandals, and a white robe. He is so much more than a man that we sing about in Sunday schools and Sunday services. He *is* the Living Word of God that became flesh and dwelt among us. He *is* the fulfillment of Genesis 3:15. He *is* the promised Seed that was prophesied to crush the serpent's head and to take back the keys to the kingdom. Hallelujah! When we see Jesus as He truly is it will be the fuel that adds fire to our worship.

I pray that you are beginning to see the correlation between Jesus as the Word of God and the Seed of the woman. There is yet another mystery to be revealed in the vast ocean of revelation that we call the Holy Bible. It can be found in Luke 8 in the Parable of the Sower. Jesus starts His parable by simply stating, *"A farmer went out to sow His seed" (v. 5).* Jesus later reveals to His disciples the mystery of the parable by plainly saying, *"The seed is the Word of God" (v. 11).*

We have already emphasized that Jesus is the Word of God but now we learn that the Word of God *is the seed of heaven!* Within the seed of God's Word is the DNA of God. Flowing within the blood of Jesus is the perfect image of the Father, the DNA of God's perfect creation. The ministry of the Holy Spirit, the gifts of prophecy and everything that proceeds from the Spirit carry the seed of the Word of God within it and is sown into the field of our hearts. We stated earlier in John 12:24 that Jesus is the seed that fell into the ground and died to bring forth much fruit. He was the seed of the woman that became the "He" of Genesis 3:15 and walked amongst us.

Everything that the Holy Spirit ministers through the gifts within us is done with one purpose; *that the Word would become flesh!* Jesus was the Firstborn amongst many brethren (Romans 8:29) and, through His death and resurrection, the same Spirit that raised Him from the dead is now poured out over all flesh. His role is to minister the Word of God to listening ears. He sows the seed of heaven on the field of our hearts that will bring forth fruit to those who receive with a believing heart. The "fruit" is the Word becoming flesh and dwelling in human vessels!

The Holy Spirit was not sent from heaven on the day of Pentecost so that we could have awesome Pentecostal/Charismatic church services, *but He was sent to testify of Jesus!* Every prophetic word, every tongue, every miracle and healing, and every other gift is given for one purpose; that the testimony of Jesus would go forth and that His Word would be sown into the hearts of mankind. *"So shall My word be that goes forth from My mouth; It shall not return to me void, but it shall accomplish what I please"* (Isaiah 55:11 NKJV). His Word is sent to become flesh within us when received by faith! True fruit is only produced when the seed of God's word takes root within us, *only when it dies within us do we bear much fruit!*

When Jesus came into the earth, He spoke in eternity saying: *"Sacrifice and offering you did not desire, but a body you have prepared for Me ... Then I said 'Here I am—It is written about Me in the scroll (the Word). I have come to do Your will Oh God."* It has always been the will of God to dwell in us. The Word of God becoming flesh is the will of God from the beginning. Jesus spoke from eternity, knowing that the will of His Father was for Him to have a body (or dwelling place) in the earth. We are His body! We are His dwelling place! His will is for us to receive His seed and, through faith and patience, allow it to bring forth fruit!

MOVING ON TO BEARING FRUIT

This entire chapter I devoted to laying the foundation for the fruit of worship. Before we continue, I want to do a simple recap of all we just read so that we can move on to bearing forth the fruit that glorifies the Father.

We learned that there is a difference between the gifts of the Spirit and the fruit of the Spirit. The gifts are given as an expression of the Spirit in our ministry to one another. These gifts are given to build one another up in the faith that we might bear fruit to the Father in our own lives. Our Father is glorified when the fruit of our lives expresses His image in all we do for Him. The fruit and character that we walk in is what blesses God Himself. It is our ministry to God. We want to be a tree that God Himself can enjoy our fruit. Unlike the fig tree that Jesus came to in His day of hunger and He could not eat from it (see Matthew 21:18-22).

It is very important that we are able to learn the difference between the gifts and the fruit before we move on. It is the revelation of the Word of God that produces the fruit. As we behold the Word of God, who is Jesus

Himself, the seed of heaven is sown into our hearts and we become like Him from glory to glory. The Word becomes flesh in us and we become living epistles written by the finger of God (see 2 Corinthians 3). Without this seed being sown we will never bring forth fruit. It is only the fruit that will remain in eternity that brings the Father glory.

It has broken my heart over the years to hear and learn about great men and women of God that have fallen from His grace. Though they produced works of ministry before the eyes of men, much like those in Matthew 7, they ceased bearing fruit in the secret place of their own hearts where the Father sees all. It has always baffled me that these men and woman could have been living in secret sin all the while their church and ministries were thriving and the Spirit was moving through them. It is this fearful reality that has been the catalyst that God has used to produce a seeking heart within me to find this revelation that I am now writing.

I honestly believe that every great leader that has fallen throughout church history started off completely sincere in their lives and ministries. I also believe that every one of us is susceptible to falling into this same trap of the enemy if we do not have a proper understanding between who we are in God (fruit) and what we do for Him (gifts).

Ultimately, we were created for worship. It is in the place of worship that we behold Him (not His works) and are transformed into that same image. The revelation of Jesus Christ is the fuel for all worship. It fuels the night and day worship that is taking place before the throne of Almighty God where mighty angels and elders bow down before Him. If we do not walk in the revelation that it is the fruit of our worship that blesses our Father, we will never move on to bearing fruit while we live here on earth. Thus we are in danger of falling from grace like those before us.

Having laid this foundation, let us now continue on to the next chapter as I expound even further in this truth. Before I move on let us pray:

Father, help us to keep our eyes on You. Lord Jesus, helps us to bear forth fruit unto You in all we do for Your kingdom. Never let us live to please ourselves, but give us Your love and Your heart to please the Father in heaven and bring forth fruit unto Him. In Jesus' name we pray. Amen.

Chapter 7

ABIDING
IN THE VINE

I am the vine, you are the branches. He who abides in Me, and I in him, bears much fruit ... By this My Father is glorified, THAT YOU BEAR MUCH FRUIT; so you will be My disciples (John 15:5,8 NKJV emphasis mine).

Sunday after Sunday I would come revved and fired up to worship God in our former church in Elk Grove, California. Some of my most memorable encounters in worship happened at the altars during those services. I can still remember moments when I literally felt at times, that if I opened my eyes, I would be flying in the air around the sanctuary. These were rapturous encounters of being caught up with Him in realms of His glory that have marked my soul for eternity. There were times when I could even hear the angelic choirs singing with us in adoration of our King.

Then there were other times, in all honesty, that I would come heavily burdened with the pressures of the prior week upon me. I would run up to the altars, clapping as loud as I could and screaming at all the wrong moments. I would do this under some false assumption that somehow if I were loud enough, God would show up like He did all the other times. It was my vain attempt to get God's attention so that I would "feel" better;

all the while I was becoming a distraction that was hindering others from connecting with God and entering into His Presence.

I thank God for the merciful pastor that I had during that time. He allowed me the grace to learn the hard way the lesson that I now have the honor of sharing with you. I was quickly becoming a "Sunday-driven" Christian that the church at large is sadly becoming. We do everything we can to build up for the Sunday morning service believing and praying that God will visit us with His Presence. The danger of this is that, in this entertainment-driven culture we live in, we can easily fall prey to the unhealthy need to be entertained. Consequently, we never allow ourselves to find satisfaction and contentment in His Presence.

Please do not misunderstand what I am saying; God is in us coming together as a corporate body. Revelation, Chapter 5, tells us of the biggest worship service of all time that takes place twenty-four hours a day, seven days a week in heaven,

> *Then I looked and heard the voice of many angels, numbering thousands upon thousands and ten thousand times ten thousand. They encircled the throne and the living creatures and elders ... fell down and worshiped* (Revelation 5:11&14).

The entire host of heaven constantly gathers around the throne of God in worship. They do not need to be entertained with bright lights and fancy buildings. They are not moved by the anointed worship-leading angels or the messengers of His word. The Presence of God Himself has captivated their attention! The thundering and the lightning that proceed from His glorious Presence create an awe inspiring worship from their innermost being. The Lord wraps Himself in light and from His being proceeds glory that will blind human eyes; just ask the apostle Paul. The Lord Himself is the object of worship in heaven and as He unveils His beauty to all the hosts of heaven, *praises ring out!* So loud is this worship that even the doorposts of heaven are shaken (see Isaiah 6)!

One of the most important lessons I learned that has set me free from so much is this: *I do not have to perform for my God!* I don't have to put on a show in my worship in order for Him to be entertained or pleased. He takes pleasure in the worship of those who are just themselves and He does not anoint men and women of God with His Spirit to entertain His people. When His people come together in perfect unity, singers and musicians, prophets and teachers, dancers and worshipers, *God will manifest His glory!* When we are all in one accord with eyes lifted up to the One who is the object of our worship, the Lord will receive the fruit of worship!

Another important truth to remember is that we were not created to *go* to church; we *are* the church. We *are* the temple of the Holy Spirit. We were not created to visit a building that we call "church." We *are* His temple built by His hands that He would abide in us and we in Him; *we are the Church of Jesus Christ!*

What immensely troubles my spirit about this generation being raised up in this entertainment-driven culture is the lack of fascination with the Presence of God. This generation gets bored quite easily if there is not a flashy show with lights and loud music. It is easy to get people to dance and shout during the fast songs, but shut down the music and just sit quietly and watch what happens. Most likely what will happen is that you will lose everybody's attention and people will get antsy and restless.

I feel strongly that a big reason this happens has to do with what I shared in Chapter 6 regarding gifts vs. fruit. We have yet to raise a generation into the mature fruit of worship. We must get past the need of being entertained through "gifted" ministries into learning how to find God for ourselves. For us to bring forth the fruit of worship to our Father we must learn the absolute need of abiding in the Vine*!*

THE LAST SUPPER

In His last night with His disciples, Jesus releases His final teaching at what has become known as the Last Supper. Now what we can learn about the Lord is that He saves the best for last; *"The last will be first and the first shall be last" (Mark 10:31).* Though it is vital to place importance on everything that Jesus taught, both to His disciples in private and to the multitudes, this particular teaching is Jesus' last night with His disciples before the crucifixion. He knew what was about to happen to Him which can tell us that He was well aware that His last words must leave the greatest impact on His chosen disciples.

In John, Chapters 13-17, we get an up close and personal look into the intimate heart of Jesus toward His disciples. It was the beginning of the Passover feast, and Jesus sent His disciples before Him to make an upper room ready so He could share this last Passover with them.

John tells us that Jesus, *"Having loved His own who were in the world, He now showed the full extent of His love" (John 13:1)*. The Amplified Bible says it this way: *"He loved them to the last and to the highest degree."* He then unclothed Himself and washed the feet of His disciples as one of the greatest acts of the servant heart of our Bridegroom King. John further tells us that Jesus knew who He was and that the Father had given Him all things.

Jesus was completely secure in His relationship with His Father. For this reason alone, He was able to humble Himself before His disciples and wash their feet. *All true ministry flows freely from the place of knowing that we are perfectly loved by our Father!* When we truly understand this, we will not have to perform for man's attention and acceptance.

After sending out Judas Iscariot (who was already filled with satan even while Jesus humbly washed his feet), the Lord then addresses His disciples. John 14-16 is one the most powerful revelations that Jesus releases to His disciples in preparing them for His departure. For the first time, Jesus begins to teach them about the person and ministry of the Holy Spirit. He spends the entire evening revealing in a whole new way His role and the role of the Holy Spirit in the Godhead. *"I am the way and the truth and the life. No one comes to the Father except through me" (John 14:6)*.

I spent the majority of Chapter 6 teaching about the gifts and ministry of the Holy Spirit and His role in revealing Jesus to us. These three chapters in the book of John reveal this truth in much more depth. Now I want to reveal how it is that we can "bear fruit" and answer the question of why it is that "fruit" brings the Father glory above the works that we do in His name.

During this last night with His beloved disciples, Jesus tells them that He is sending the Holy Spirit to teach them all things and bring all His words to their remembrance. He even blows their minds by saying, *"Most assuredly, I say to you, he who believes in Me, the works that I do he will do also; and greater works than these he will do, because I go to My Father"* *(John 14:12 NKJV).* Absolutely mind- blowing! Greater works than those of Jesus? Because He was going to be with the Father, the Spirit in them would bear witness to Christ by confirming their words with signs following them. But, much like Paul's teaching to the Corinthian church on the gifts of the Spirit, Jesus sandwiched this teaching in between His unveiling of the ministry of the Holy Spirit:

> *I am the true vine, and My Father is the vinedresser. Every branch in Me that does not bear fruit He takes away; and every branch that bears fruit He prunes, that it may bear more fruit ... Abide in Me, and I in you. As the branch cannot bear fruit of itself, unless it abides in the vine, neither can you unless you abide in Me* (John 15:1-2;4 NKJV).

Jesus finishes this by saying, *"By this My Father is glorified, that you bear much fruit; so you will be my disciples" (v. 8).*

This statement is profound to me. Jesus ends His earthly ministry after three and one half years of shaking the nation of Israel with signs, wonders, and miracles. These miracles spoke to Israel, declaring Him to be Messiah. He speaks to His disciples regarding the importance of His departure so that they, too, can receive the Holy Spirit. He tells them that, because of the Spirit, they will do even greater works of ministry than He did. Praise God! For any lover of Jesus this is a Scripture that grips your heart. I am longing to see signs, wonders, and miracles break out in the streets of our cities like in the days of Jesus and the apostles. In fact, signs will follow ALL who believe, not just apostles and preachers.

What Jesus is doing here is establishing a precedent for the future ministry of the church. He was essentially telling them: *"You guys are going to shake the world when I leave. I am looking forward to this time as I go to be with My Father because the Holy Spirit will come and be in you like He is in Me. But what you must also understand is that it is when you bear fruit that My Father is glorified!*

To help establish this teaching, Jesus had just said to them, *"A new command I give you: Love one another. As I have loved you, so you must love one another. By this everyone will know that you are My disciples, if you love one another" (John 13:34).*

Take note that Jesus did not say that it is by the signs, wonders, and miracles that follow us that will show the world we are His disciples *but by our love or "fruit" that we bear!* The fruit of righteousness and the selfless love of God that we bear in us are what bring the Father glory.

WHY FRUIT?

Now why is this? Why is it fruit that glorifies the Father? Don't His mighty works declare His glory? Why is it that Jesus emphatically makes a distinction between what we do *through* the Holy Spirit and who we are in the Father? I believe it is for this one reason: *"I am the Lord, that is My name! I will not give my glory to another or my praise to idols" (Isaiah 42:8).* The Lord is jealous for His glory and He will not share it with man. Yet, in His loving kindness, He shares the glory of His Presence with sons and daughters. Psalm 8 even tells us that He has, *"...made him (man) a little lower than the angels"* yet He *"has crowned him with GLORY and honor (v.5 NKJV)."* What is this? One Scripture says that He will not give His glory to another, yet another says that He has crowned man with glory and honor. Let me expound a little on this.

God knows what is in the heart of man! Time after time Jesus would withdraw Himself from the crowds.

Many people saw the miraculous signs He was doing and believed in His name. But Jesus would not entrust Himself to them, for He knew all men. He did not need man's testimony about man, for He knew what was in a man (John 2:23-25).

As the people witnessed His miracles they even wanted to take Him *by force* to make Him king.

So what is it about man that Jesus knew was in them? I believe the answer to this is very simple; *the love of self or pride!* Our self-will and pride will always war against the will of God. The "fruit" of sin and pride is love for self but the fruit of the Spirit is love for God; *perfect love* that casts out fear. Fear is rooted in love for self. If you love yourself more than you love God, then your fear will always war against the Spirit of God. As a result (or the "fruit"), we will refuse to let go of the control of our own lives. By our own "self-will" we end up living contrary to the will of God.

We see this example in the life of Jesus in the garden of Gethsemane. In His hour of temptation we see the war inside His soul to save His own life. Finally, *through prayer,* He broke through His "self" and declared, *"Father, not My will, but Yours be done!" (Mark 14:36).*

This is why I believe that Jesus teaches strongly that it is fruit in our lives that glorifies the Father and the love for one another that shows the world that we are His disciples. Jesus was given the Spirit without measure. He walked in the fullness of the Godhead within His body. But it was the fruit of His character that refused to let His own will dictate how He used this authority handed to Him by the Father. He walked in perfect love for His Father and He did only what pleased Him. Jesus was fully God *but He was also FULLY MAN!* He was tempted in all points that we ourselves are tempted. He battled the same temptations to live for Himself just like we do. Yet, through His life of submission, He demonstrated to us that we can do the works of God and not be lifted up in pride! This is why "fruit" glorifies the Father. Yes, His works through us are signs that point to a greater reality; *a life lived IN LOVE with God and our brothers and sisters.*

The Lord is well acquainted with the pride of the sinful nature. *"Pride comes before destruction" (Proverbs 16:18).* He loves us so much and does not want to see us go down that path that ends in destruction. The Lord has seen the pride of Lucifer, the anointed cherub, who even walked in the midst of the stones of fire. Because he was gifted above most others, Lucifer was lifted up in pride. Jesus even made the statement, *"I saw Satan fall like lightning from heaven."* God will not share His glory with pride. He has already seen the fruit of Lucifer's sin as he drew away a third of the angels with him as they were thrust out from His Presence forever. He loves us too much to see us fall into the same condemnation.

God gives to us the same Spirit that was in Christ. He equips us to do the same miracles and even greater works. He sends us into this dying world and commands us to *"Heal the sick, raise the dead, cleanse those who have leprosy, drive out demons. Freely you have received, freely give"* *(Matthew 10:8).* The first disciples went out after Jesus' commission and came back astonished because of the miracles that they were performing through His name. In reply to their reaction He says,

> *I have given you authority to trample on snakes and scorpions and to overcome ALL the power of the enemy; nothing will harm you. However, do not rejoice that the spirits submit to you, but rejoice that your names are written in heaven* (Luke 10:18-20 emphasis mine).

Jesus gives this commission to His disciples in the early days. Then, on the last night of His ministry on earth, with His chosen disciples He releases this command, *"A new command I give you: Love one another. As I have loved you, so you must love one another" (John 13:34).* Love is the end of the commandment! Perfect, selfless love *is* the fruit of a heart that has been saved from the pride of the sinful nature.

Now, having said all this, let me bring this all around. *Jesus is not disannulling His command of Matthew 10:8 and doing the "greater works"—* just as Paul was not telling the Corinthians to quench the ministry of the Holy Spirit, but simply said to them, "And now I will show you the most excellent way" (1 Corinthians 12:31), which is the way of love. If we have received the baptism of fire, then we should be seeing the signs, wonders, and miracles. I am not teaching that we need to stop seeking after the power of God manifesting in signs and miracles. It is the will of God that we see His power in operation every day and in every area of our lives. The only reason that we are not seeing the power of God in full operation in America is that we have settled for a form of godliness but denied the power (see 2 Timothy 3:4-5). Paul tells us that this form of Christianity is lived by those who are *"lovers of pleasure (self) more than lovers of God."*

As we fulfill the command to love God and love one another, then signs *will* follow behind us as we fan the flames of perfect love. God will get the glory that is His through the "works" that manifest by the power of His Spirit in us. To His glory, we will bear fruit that remains because we will not be lifted up in pride thereby falling from grace.

ABIDING IN THE VINE

Now back to John 15. Jesus has taught His disciples about the coming of the Holy Spirit and His indwelling Presence. I can just see the anticipation in their hearts; captivated by every word that has proceeded from the God-Man Jesus Christ. They have fallen head over heels in love with this Man that they believe to be Messiah. He tells them "I'm going away, but I'm sending the Holy Spirit and He will teach you all things."

During this time, Jesus picked up on the sadness of their hearts because He told them that He was going away. They had lived in the constant Presence of Jesus for three and a half years. They had even been used by the Lord to do miracles through His name. It is here that Jesus chooses to reveal to His disciples how they can be with Him, even in His absence. Understand that the disciples, at this point, have no idea that Jesus is trying to convey to them, "I'm about to be crucified, but don't worry." He says to them, *"Abide in me, and I in you" (John 15:4 NKJV).* The NIV puts it this way *"Remain in Me."* This word might be a better translation of the Greek word "meno" which means "to remain, abide, and dwell (endure or last."1 For this word I will now use both "abide and remain" and I will explain later.

Abiding in Him is an absolute essential to our walk in this world. Jesus is telling us right here how to make it. "*Abide in Me!* Don't just visit Me on Sunday morning. Don't just visit Me in your time of need; *abide and remain in Me!* Only as you abide and remain in Me will you bear fruit that will bring glory to My Father."

There were times during the ministry of Jesus that His disciples would

115

get so busy doing *for* Jesus that they would leave His Presence. A great example of this is when Jesus had just fed the multitude in John 6. Having escaped the crowd's desire to take Him by force and make Him king, Jesus withdrew to a mountain place to commune with the Father. In Matthew's account, he tells us that Jesus even told His disciples to get on the boat and go ahead of Him while He dismissed the crowds. Now His disciples obediently get into the boat and start rowing to the other side. There is only one problem; *they left without Jesus!* After this a storm breaks out and Jesus comes walking on the water and saves them as He always did faithfully.

I believe this is such a picture of many today who leave "abiding and remaining" in His Presence to do the work of the Lord. Many of these people see the results because they were once in His Presence, but they are in danger of losing the heart that desires only Him. A heart that does *for* God without being motivated by perfect love can easily fall into pride.

You might be saying, "Wait a minute, the disciples were being obedient!" That is true, they were following orders. I believe this was a test for His disciples, just as I believe the Lord will test us all in our walk with Him. Will we run ahead of God and be busy with ministry in His name or will we choose "abiding and remaining" in His Presence? Before you turn your ears off and deem me a heretic and false teacher, let me give you evidence to what I am saying.

Let's take Moses as an Old Testament example. The Lord told Moses from His mouth, *"Leave this place, you and the people ... and go to the land I promised ... I will send an angel before you ... But I WILL NOT GO WITH YOU." (Exodus 33:1-3 emphasis mine).* Yet Moses refused the command of God and said, *"If Your Presence does not go with us, do not send us up from here"* (v. 15). Now was Moses being defiant to God? Was he in rebellion in by refusing the direct instruction of the Lord? I mean, really you guys, who would dare speak to God like this? But listen to God's response, *"I will do the very thing you have asked, because I am pleased with you and I know you by name"* (v. 17).

Moses established such a relationship with God through "abiding and remaining" in His Presence that he refused to do ANYTHING without His Presence being priority. He even abode so much in His Presence that his face shone from the glory of God. The Lord even declared to Moses *"I know you by name,"* unlike those in Matthew 7 when Jesus will say on the Day of Judgment, *"I never KNEW you."*

Let me now jump into the New Testament and give you further example showing how the Lord will test us to reveal the true pursuit of our heart. In Luke 10:38-42, Jesus is in the house of Lazarus, Martha, and Mary in the city of Bethany. As always, Jesus sat and taught. Martha became upset because she was busy trying to serve while her sister Mary sat at the feet of Jesus to listen to His word. Martha was serving the guests and had what seemed to be a legitimate complaint against her sister. After all, the work of the ministry has to continue right? Martha then complains to the Lord and asks Him to tell Mary to get up and help. Listen to Jesus' response. *"Martha, Martha, you are worried and upset about many things, but only one thing is needed. Mary has chosen what is better, and it will not be taken from her."*

David says in Psalm 27:4, "One thing I ask of the Lord, this is what I seek: That I may dwell [abide, remain] *in the house of the Lord all the days of my life, to gaze upon the beauty of the Lord and to seek Him in His temple."* David was called by God Himself "a man after My own heart." All he wanted was to dwell, abide, and remain in the house of the Lord. This Old Testament passage speaking of the "house" signifies the New Testament reality of the Presence of God. Even later in David's life, when Absalom attempted to take the kingdom away from his father, David only longed for the ark (Presence). He was willing to give up all the stuff; *it was Presence that His heart longed for!* Moses, David, and Mary all chose presence above ministry! So must we choose the "one thing" desire to worship in His Presence before all else. All ministry that is done from this place of being "Presence-centered" will glorify God.

The Presence of God MUST be priority number one in the life of every believer. True worship comes forth *in His Presence!* The Presence of God is the "one thing that is needed." The Father receives the fruit of true worship as we "abide and remain" in His Presence. Choosing His Presence before anything else is the key to bearing fruit that will remain in eternity as we stand before His throne.

I mentioned earlier that the word "remain" is a more accurate translation, and here is why. What Jesus is trying to clarify more clearly is, "Endure, last, and remain in Me; *don't give up!* My Father will prune you back so that you can keep bearing more fruit. Life will throw everything at you. The enemy is going to want to take you out, but *remain in Me* and you will glorify My Father through the fruit that comes up from your life of worship!"

I believe this passage to be one of the most revealing statements in our need for worship. Putting Presence first is how we abide and remain in Him. Through every trial in life, when you are driven by Presence, you will endure. When we can get into the Presence of God and behold Him, our worship allows us to cast aside every other care in this life and "choose what is needed." Our worship produces within us fruit that will remain. The fruit of our worship will endure the temptation to give up or to be lifted up in pride. The Presence of God is the driving force that keeps us centered in the throne room of heaven. Nothing else will satisfy but to behold the beauty of the Lord in the secret place of the Most High God.

The fruit of worship is a son or daughter who will abide and remain in His Presence all the days of their life. No weapon formed against them will prosper because nothing will separate them from the love relationship they have with their Bridegroom King. This fruit brings glory to the Father because a burning heart will not be enticed to take His glory from Him through its ministry accomplishments. The fruit of our labor for God will never supersede the fruit of a life of worship because we are driven into His Presence through desire for Him. Even if God sends us out on an assignment, we will never leave His Presence, because our desire burns for Him to go with us; if He doesn't go with us, then we won't go. This is the fruit of worship! This is to the glory of the Father. He will entrust greater authority to these who bear the fruit of worship because they will not bow down to the god of this world and cast this crown at his feet; *they cast their crowns at the feet of King Jesus only. HALLELUJAH. This is why we were created!*

ABIDING IN THE VINE

THE HIGHEST FORM OF WORSHIP

Before I finish this portion of the book I want to bring everything around full circle. True worship produces obedience; *the highest form of worship is obedience!*

Jesus sums up His teaching about being the True Vine and the importance of us, as the branches, abiding in Him by saying,

> *As the Father has loved me, so have I loved you. Now remain in my love. If you obey my commands, you will remain in my love, just as I have obeyed my Father's command and remain in his love* (John 15:9-10).

God has created every living thing with the purpose that we would abide and remain in Him; *this is true worship.* Through this life of abiding in Him we will become vessels who do His bidding, NOT BECAUSE WE HAVE TO, BUT BECAUSE IT BECOMES OUR DESIRE AND PLEASURE TO PLEASE OUR FATHER! This is the fruit of worship: *A life who finds pleasure in obeying God.* Even in our obedience, we never leave His Presence because we are IN LOVE! Let me say this again, when you are in love, YOU NEVER LEAVE HIS PRESENCE BECAUSE YOU DWELL IN HIM AND HE IS IN YOU.

Dead religion has put worship into this box of songs that we sing in a building on Sunday mornings. Yet all the while, many people's hearts are far from God during this time of our "worship services." God is not IN them and they are not IN Him. Dead religion has turned being obedient into following a set of rules and calling that "holiness." NO! A thousand times NO! True worship produces within us the fruit to do the Father's will with absolute joy and gladness. Obedience becomes the pleasure of our lives when you are madly in love with God. God is IN obedience. His Presence dwells IN truth because His word IS truth.

True worship ultimately produces a son or a daughter of the Most High God that is IN LOVE with their Father and their Bridegroom Jesus.

When you are in love, obedience isn't a duty, it is a pleasure. You will be driven with absolute passion for the Presence of the Lord and thus you will do whatever it takes to please Him and to "keep" His Presence with you. Perfect love is selfless; it takes no pleasure in pleasing self, but only in pleasing the Lord. This is the fruit of abiding in HIS love. God is perfect love. It is only as we abide in Him that we will become like Him in our love. The highest form of worship is obedience.

Unfortunately, in the church today, obedience has been deemed as some religious, legalistic word that scares people away. This has happened because of insecure leaders that have used their authority to manipulate people to do their will, not the will of God. Yet, we *must* redeem the importance of obedience in the lives of His children.

The truth of the matter is that it is absolutely impossible to obey God in the sinful nature. Without being born again and receiving a DNA change within us, we will forever live for ourselves. Obedience is a bad word to religious people who live for themselves. Yet now, because of the grace of God imparted to us by faith, we can do His will *by nature. This is true worship!* Apart from Him we can do nothing. Yet, because He abides in us and we remain in Him, we will, *by nature,* live in obedience. It's just the way God created things.

Everything in creation moves in obedience to what God has commanded from the beginning. Not because they have to, but because it is *in* them to follow His will. Even the angels obey God:

Praise the Lord, you His angels, you mighty ones who do His bidding, who obey His word. Praise the Lord, all His heavenly hosts, you servants who do His will. Praise the Lord all His works, everywhere in His dominion (Psalm 103:20-22).

The sun, the moon, and all the stars obey His voice. All creation obeys His command. Obedience is the highest form of worship because obedience is the natural response of the created being to the command of God. When God speaks from His throne, obedience follows the breath of His word wherever the Spirit goes.

Obedience will cease to be a bad religious word when we fall in love. This is why I so fervently believe that worship is key. Worship is the key that unlocks the everlasting gates of the heavenly realms and lets the King of glory invade the earth. Everything that I have written about in previous chapters—the heart, the place, the object, the fragrance, and the fruit of worship—all point us to a life-long journey of falling in love. When all is said and done; all the suffering and all the highs and lows of life are simply preparation for a wedding; the marriage between the Lamb of God Jesus and His bride, the church.

Jesus tells us, *"If you love me, you will keep my commands" (John 14:15)*. Religion has taken this Scripture and attempted to bind the people of God. As if we need to prove our love for God by keeping His commands. It is IMPOSSIBLE to keep the commands of God without His grace! We will never keep the commands of God if we are not in love. What Jesus is really saying here is, "When you are in love, you will keep My commands." Love is the end of the command. The command ceases being a grievous "command" when you are in love. It becomes the pleasure of worship to obey His every word.

I pray that the Lord has opened your spiritual eyes to grasp and comprehend the greatness of His love towards you. In return, I pray that you would pour out that same love toward Him; this is true worship! Giving back to God the same love that He has first given to us! Now let us move on into part two and the end time army that God is raising up in this last hour before His return.

Part Two

THE END TIME ARMY

Chapter 8

THE DAVIDIC GENERATION

After removing Saul, He made David their king. God testified concerning him: "I have found David son of Jesse a man after My own heart; he will do everything I want him to do (Acts 13:22).

n John 4:23-24, Jesus spoke to the woman at the well saying,

A time is coming and has now come when the true worshipers will worship the Father in Spirit and truth, for they are the kind of worshipers the Father seeks. God is Spirit, and His worshipers must worship in spirit and in truth.

This word that Jesus spoke has been the catalyst that has fueled my pursuit in seeking what exactly the Father is looking for in a worshiper. True worshipers are what the Father is seeking after.

The Father is not looking for true apostles and prophets. He is not looking for true ministers or preachers. He is not looking for true megachurches to be established. *He is looking for true worshipers!*

The first part of this book was an in-depth look into true worship. Though I barely scratched the surface of the glory of what true worship entails, I pray that the spirit of revelation has opened your eyes to see what God is saying to us. It is the Lord's will for us to be able to grasp the unsearchable riches of His glory. From this place of revelation, true worship comes forth.

I am now going to dedicate the rest of this book into revealing some aspects of the End Time Army that God is raising up in this hour. This is the army that is in the forefront of this battle that is preparing the earth for the second coming of Jesus Christ and His millennial reign.

2 Chronicles 16:9 says: *"For the eyes of the Lord run to and fro throughout the whole earth, to show Himself strong on behalf of those whose heart is loyal to Him" (NKJV).* Our God is a passionate seeker! Even in the garden of Eden He came "looking" for Adam and Eve saying, "Where are you?" In His encounter with the woman at the well, Jesus reveals to us all what the Father is seeking; *true worshipers.*

In our pursuit of looking at the End Time Army we must begin with David. I believe him to be the greatest example because God Himself bore witness that he was "a man after My own heart." So great was this man in the eyes of the Lord that He chose to bring His Son into the world through his lineage. So great, in fact, that our Lord Jesus was called "Son of David."

ISRAEL SOUGHT FOR A MAN

In the days of the prophet Samuel, Israel became discontented with the prophetic leadership that the Lord had placed them under. They became envious of the nations around them as they witnessed their kings leading them out to battle. In their envy they approached Samuel and demanded a king to be appointed over them that they may be like the other nations. When Samuel brought their request before the Lord, He responded by saying: *"Listen to all that the people are saying to you; it is not you they have rejected, but they have rejected me as their king" (1 Samuel 8:7).*

The Lord granted to Israel what they desired. In their rejection of the prophetic leadership, they sought for a man to lead them. God sent Samuel to the tribe of Benjamin and chose Saul the son of Kish to be anointed the first king of Israel. The Bible tells us that he was *"an impressive young*

THE DAVIDIC GENERATION

man without equal among the Israelites – a head taller than any of the others" (1 Samuel 9:2).

Israel was granted the king that they desired. He led them in and out of their battles and they rejoiced greatly in his strength. Saul gained great favor with the people through his public victories. In the eyes of Israel, Saul was God's man. He was anointed by Samuel before the entire nation and he stood head and shoulders above the rest. It only seemed to make perfect sense that the man who stood out amongst the rest must be the greatest in Israel.

When we are not founded upon faith in God and completely surrendered to His will, we will walk by sight and not by faith. Saul appeared to be the best man for the job, yet God does not see as man sees; He looks into the heart. God gave to Israel what they asked because they sought for a man to lead them the way they believed leadership should look.

Oftentimes God will give us what we ask though it's not what He desires for us. God, in His wisdom, allowed Israel to have the king that they desired. He knew, and even told them before hand, that Saul would afflict His people. For us to gain a greater understanding of the Davidic generation in this end time army I believe we must also take a good look into the life of Saul.

I believe the end times will look much like this era in Israel's history. In the Hebraic culture, the era of Eli and his sons was considered one of their darkest hours as a nation. The lamp of God was no longer burning and the people were being seduced by the sons of Eli, even to the point that his sons were sleeping with the women who ministered at the doorway of the tabernacle. Samuel is considered a type of redeemer and savior to the children of Israel. He was a Nazirite from birth and in his growth as a man of God, the Word of the Lord was with him. He brought reformation to the entire nation and began to fervently teach the nation the ways of the Lord. *Yet the people of God rejected the prophetic office and the voice of the Lord!* In their rejection of the prophetic voice they demanded that a "man" lead them into victory over their enemies. The people of God rejected the kingdom of heaven and asked for a political regime, led by a man as their king, to rule over them.

Do you see the correlation here in regard to the last days? Scripture tells us that a "man" will rise up in the end times and all humanity will look to him for leadership. Again, the Hebraic culture teaches that the Messiah will come in the last hour as a conquering king to defeat the enemies of the Lord and set up His kingdom on the Earth. As I shared earlier in Chapters 6 and 7, the Holy Spirit within us will testify to the life of Jesus. All Old Testament Scriptures are types and shadows that testify beforehand to the life, death and resurrection of Jesus Christ and the kingdom of God. I say this to establish the foundation to where I am taking us, as I reveal this end time Davidic generation that God is raising up on the earth.

THE REGIME OF KING SAUL

The regime of Saul was allowed by God to rule over Israel in response to their cry for a king. Again, we must see that God was the One that sent Samuel to find Saul. Oftentimes, because we do not understand the sovereignty of God, we can erroneously believe that the devil is getting one over on God. In this end time generation, the rise of antichrist will not catch God off guard. Everything that happens on the earth will be allowed by God to fulfill His purpose when all is said and done. In the book of Revelation you will consistently read: "and to them it was given." This statement is made regarding those through whom much of the evil will happen in the last hour. Now let me ask this; who is the One "giving to them" the authority to do what they are doing? The answer is God! God is sovereign all by Himself. This simply means that He is supreme ruler of all, *"For there is no authority except from God, and the authorities that exist are appointed by God" (Romans 13:1 NKJV).*

It is very important that we have a firm foundation in who our God is. When we are founded in the knowledge of the sovereignty of God then we also understand that whatever schemes or devices that the enemy throws against us God can use for His glory. The devil, in all his subtleties and craftiness, will play right into the hands of our all wise God.

Again, I am stating all of this to lay the foundation for this Davidic Generation and the regime of Saul. This regime played a key role in the

THE DAVIDIC GENERATION

preparation of the reign of David, much like the rise of antichrist in this last hour will play its role in preparing the earth for the second coming of Christ. Christ is coming to reign on the throne of David!

The life of Saul truly is a sad story. Saul started out a sincere, godly man that even exuded great humility. When Samuel called him to the feast, Saul responded, *"But am I not a Benjamite, from the smallest tribe of Israel ... Why do you say such a thing to me?" (1 Samuel 9:21).* When Saul was anointed king he simply went home and didn't mention a word to anyone but kept the matter to himself. Even at his inauguration he hid himself in the luggage when he was called by Samuel to be anointed before the people.

So, how could this man who began his reign over Israel in great humility end up having murdered eighty-five priests of the Lord, pursuing David with the intent to kill him, and even consulting witches? The answer to this question is quite simple; *disobedience!* The more that I study the life of Saul, the more I see a sincere man that simply fell short of obeying the Lord *to completion.*

Let me now take us on a journey through the Scripture. As we read these accounts, notice the key statement "to completion." It's not that Saul was outright rebellious and obstinate; he just failed to obey to completion.

In 1 Samuel 13, we read that in the second year of Saul's reign he went out to battle against the Philistines. Scripture tells us that there were three thousand chariots, six thousand horsemen, and soldiers as numerous as the sand that is on the seashore that were gathered against Israel. Saul was given specific instruction by Samuel to wait seven days at Gilgal until his arrival. Day after day the Israelites looked upon the armies of the enemy and they were filled with fear. Saul's army slowly dwindled down to a small remnant of trembling soldiers.

In all honesty, it really appears that Saul was obedient. He waited until the seventh day as he was instructed. In an extreme moment of pressure, Saul looked at his trembling soldiers and finally took it upon himself to offer the sacrifice. Immediately after he did this, Samuel appeared. Saul did everything he could to last the full seven days, *yet at the last minute he caved under the pressure!* He did not obey to completion. He made it

129

ninety-nine percent of the way yet, at the last moment, he disobeyed the instruction of the Lord. Deep down he wanted to obey but he did not have the character to see it through until the end.

So what was it about Saul's actions that God rejected? Is not our God forgiving? Why would the Lord not give Saul another opportunity? Didn't Saul do everything within him to wait the full seven days? The answer is yes, God is forgiving and merciful. Yes, Saul did do everything he could to wait. Many of us would have caved the same way. Let's look carefully though at Saul's reasoning for not obeying to completion:

When I saw that the men were scattering, and that YOU DID NOT COME AT THE SET TIME, and that the Philistines were assembling at Micmash, I thought, "Now the Philistines will come down against me at Gilgal, AND I HAVE NOT SOUGHT THE LORD'S FAVOR." So I felt compelled to offer the burnt offering (1 Samuel 13:11-12).

In his heart he convinced himself that he was doing this for God and refused to take responsibility for his disobedience. Notice how he put it off on Samuel for not arriving at the appointed time.

This situation can very much mirror Adam and Eve in the garden of Eden. God, in His mercy, will always plead with us in our disobedience. Yet pride will refuse to confess in the moment of conviction and confrontation. Adam even blamed the Lord saying, *"The woman You gave me made me eat."* Then Eve, in her opportunity to confess, blamed the serpent.

Saul, like Adam and Eve, was given an opportunity to repent. Unfortunately, like them, he pointed the blame toward another. I'm sure the men around him really applauded his religiosity in putting the Lord first and offering the sacrifice himself; *yet in his religious ways he cast off obedience!* A religious spirit will always clothe itself with the pride of doing God's will outwardly in the eyes of man, yet God sees the motives of the heart. Had Saul simply confessed his sin and repented, we might have a different story today.

THE DAVIDIC GENERATION

There are many who may not know this, but it was this simple act of disobedience *and* the lack of repentance that cost Saul the kingdom. Upon Samuel's arrival to Gilgal, he rebuked Saul and spoke this to him: *"The Lord has sought out a man after His own heart and appointed him leader of His people, because you have not kept the Lord's command"* (1 Samuel 13:14).

Next, let's take a look at 1 Samuel 14. The Philistines again camp against Israel to war against them. Saul's son, Jonathan, along with his armor bearer, valiantly approach the Philistine camp and single-handedly begin routing the enemy. During this time, Saul has the entire army of Israel take a religious oath to not eat until the Lord would avenge him of his enemies.

Saul's proud, religious ways have now begun to bring distress upon the entire army. His faithful men have now bound themselves under an oath that God was not calling them to. Religion always binds the people of God under commands, but never carries with it the grace to follow through to completion!

Saul was a religious man that won the favor of the people, but lost the favor of God. The grace of God *is* His divine favor. Understand this about religion; *it has all the outward displays of doing the will of God, but the heart motive is rooted in the will of "self"!*

The men of Israel were under this religious leadership of Saul. For this reason they did not have the grace to follow through with Saul's command and they lustfully slew animals in their hunger and ate the meat with the blood. Saul sees this sin and, in his religious zeal, builds his first altar to the Lord and inquires of God. It later becomes revealed to Saul that Jonathan (who was unaware of this oath because he was fighting the Lord's battle) had eaten honey after the victory. Again, Saul in his religious zeal, attempts to kill his own son for breaking the command that he placed upon the people. Saul was even willing to kill his own son even though the Lord had used him to fight his battles for him. This is exactly what religion does; *it kills in the name of the Lord!*

Last of all, let's take a look into the account of 1 Samuel 15. This is the situation that most will recall as Saul's disobedience that caused him to have the kingdom stripped from him. Samuel comes to Saul and instructs him from the Lord to go to battle against the Amalekites as an act of judgment against them for their treatment of Israel hundreds of years earlier when God brought them out of Egypt. Samuel again gives to him very specific instructions:

Now go, attack the Amalekites and totally destroy everything that belongs to them. Do not spare them; put to death men and women, children and infants, cattle and sheep, camels and donkeys (1 Samuel 15:3).

I want us to take note that Saul does not look to Samuel and say, "No! I won't do it. I refuse!" Instead he instantly responds, musters up the army and attacks Amalek even as Samuel spoke to him. He killed all the people but spared Agag, the king, and the best of the animals. After this, the word of the Lord came to Samuel, *"I am grieved that I have made Saul king, because he has turned away from me and has not carried out My instructions" (v. 11).* Saul truly believed that he had carried out the instruction of God. Even when Samuel approached him, Saul said, *"The Lord bless you! I have carried out the Lord's instructions" (v. 13).* In the eyes of Israel, Saul was a great king that was always putting the Lord first. Even in his defense to Samuel's rebuke he says, *"But I did obey the Lord ... I went on the mission the Lord assigned me ... The soldiers took sheep and cattle from the plunder, THE BEST OF WHAT WAS DEVOTED TO GOD, IN ORDER TO SACRIFICE THEM TO THE LORD YOUR GOD AT GILGAL" (vv. 20-21 emphasis mine).*

Saul believed with all his heart that he was following the Lord, yet when Samuel finds him he is building a monument in his own honor! Oh, how much does this sound like today. So many running around building ministries in the name of the Lord, but when it all boils down to it they are building monuments in honor of themselves.

Saul's confession reveals the true motive behind it all: *"I violated the Lord's command and your instructions. I WAS AFRAID OF THE PEOPLE AND SO I GAVE INTO THEM" (v. 24 emphasis mine).* As Samuel turns to

THE DAVIDIC GENERATION

leave, Saul begs him, *"Please honor me before the elders of my people and before Israel; come back with me, so that I may worship the Lord your God"* *(v. 30)*. Here is where we see the root of it all; the fear of man and the love of self which will always manifest as a man-pleasing spirit! Because Saul did not have a genuine fear of God. He cared more about what others thought than what God thought. Though he carried within him a genuine desire to serve the Lord, his fear of what others thought prevented him from carrying out obedience to completion. This kind of man-pleasing heart always opens the door to the spirit of religion.

Some of you might be asking, "What does this mean for us today?" Glad you asked! The regime of Saul is a picture for us of a political regime with a religious leader. Political correctness has become the voice of much of society at large and has crept in like cancer into the church. The political spirit is motivated in pleasing man more than God and thus will not obey God to completion. The Pharisees followed in this exact lifestyle when Jesus confronted them for loving the praises of man more than God. They were obedient in paying their tithes, teaching from the Law of Moses, and praying in public places, but Jesus said that they omitted the "weightier matters" of justice, faith and mercy.

The apostle Paul talks of the last days and the people who *"...will not endure sound doctrine, but according to their own desires, because they have itching ears, they will heap up for themselves teachers"* *(2 Timothy 4:3 NKJV)*. This is exactly what Israel did in the hour of Samuel's leadership. In fact, Israel continued in this sin leading right up to the first coming of Christ. The prophetic voice of God was not telling them what they wanted to hear, so they shut off their ears from hearing God and "heaped" up leaders who would give them what they wanted and tell them what they wanted to hear. Even today, many pastors and leaders have to live in fear that they can be voted out of their congregations if they are not pleasing the people.

Understand that Saul was not a heathen king, meaning one who did not believe in the Lord God of Israel. Israel did not cast away the Lord as their God and ask for an unbeliever to lead them. They just wanted someone who would do what they wanted him to do. Saul was a man who

133

followed the Lord, just not with his whole heart. Caring more about what people thought allowed fear to creep in, and fear will always hold us back from obeying to completion. This is the fruit of dead religion. The regime of Saul becomes a picture of religious leadership that outwardly, in the public places, does all the right things and does just enough to make men happy in themselves. The Pharisees followed the same pattern in the days of the first coming of Jesus Christ. So will it be in this hour as the world prepares for the second coming.

Some of the most evil regimes in modern history have come to leadership under the banner of Christianity. Adolf Hitler rose up in Germany and deceived an entire nation. The church hailed him as God's answer to the needs of His people. Yet when the curtains fell, six million Jews were exterminated behind closed doors. Even in America today, we are witnessing the killing of unborn babies in the name of women's rights. The humanistic agenda that is on the rise in our nation has all the outward appearance of godly love and truth, yet the Spirit of God and all creation are groaning under the grief that we have cast off the ways of the Lord.

THE LORD HAS SOUGHT OUT A MAN

Saul's life is one of the saddest stories in the Bible. I believe there is a very important reason why the Word of God devotes such a portion to his life. This is also the reason that I have devoted a portion of this chapter to study his account. We started off by looking into 1 Samuel 13 and the simple act of disobedience that cost him the kingdom. Saul did not start off killing eighty-five priests of the Lord or chasing after David to murder him. He did not start out consulting witches; *he simply disobeyed the instruction of the Lord and refused to repent!* This is what cost him the kingdom.

In response to Saul's act of disobedience and lack of repentance, Samuel reveals to him the heart of God:

You have not kept the command the Lord your God gave you; if you had, he would have established your kingdom over Israel for all time. But now your kingdom will not endure; THE LORD HAS

SOUGHT A MAN AFTER HIS OWN HEART and appointed him leader of His people (1 Samuel 13:13-14 emphasis mine).

From this time forward, God began to lift His hand from Saul's life. Even before David was born, God knew who he was and prepared Israel for his leadership. This incident of Gilgal in 1 Samuel 13 happened during the second year of Saul's reign as king. We know that Saul reigned for forty years. Simple math tells us this incident was thirty-eight years old before David became king. David was thirty years old when he took the throne. This incident happened eight years before David was born. So again, we could say that before David was ever in his mother's womb, he was chosen by God.

The nation of Israel had to again endure a forty-year transitional period. Much like the forty-year wilderness trials, Israel as a nation was in preparation for the promise of God.

While Israel was under the harsh leadership of Saul, God found a man named David in the sheep fields tending his father's flock. All the while he was worshiping and cultivating an intimate relationship with the Lord God of Israel. Though Israel was beneath the tyranny of the regime of Saul, David remained hidden in the secret place of the Most High and found grace in the eyes of the Lord.

God Himself testified of David and called him a "man after my own heart." The Lord sought out a man and, in John 4, Jesus revealed what it is the Lord seeks. He seeks worshipers; *He found David!* Even in the oppressive era of severe war against the Philistines, David was abiding in the field singing love songs to the Lord on his harp. God found a man after His own heart; He found a worshiper! Though David was a mighty warrior, it was his intimate heart that burned in love for God that won him favor in the eyes of the Lord. Yes, David could slay his ten thousands, but it was his love for the presence of God that moved the heart of God. It was his addiction to the place of worship that the Lord found in him to be a man after His own heart. I say often: The greatest warriors are the most intimate worshipers!

Israel sought out a man that had all the outward appearance of a champion. The Lord sought out a man and found David to be His champion because of his simple life of worship. In the secret place of his heart, David was in love with God. That is what God sees! Even Samuel, when he was sent to David's father's household, looked at the outward appearance of David's eldest brother Eliab. Listen to God's response:

Do not consider his appearance or his height, for I have rejected him. The Lord does not look at the things man looks at. Man looks at the outward appearance, but the Lord looks at the heart (1 Samuel 16:7).

In this last hour we also cannot look at the outward appearance as man sees. In the book of Revelation, John saw the beast *"rising out of the sea" (Revelation 13:1 NKJV),* implying a gradual uprising into a place of power. The same apostle wrote in 1 John 4:3:

Every spirit that does not acknowledge Jesus is not from God. This is the spirit of the antichrist, which you have heard is coming AND EVEN NOW IS ALREADY IN THE WORLD (emphasis mine).

John is telling us over 1900 years ago that the spirit of antichrist is already in the world! When we stop looking for a "man" then God will open our eyes to see how He sees.

The entire nation of Israel was looking for a "man." David was looking for God! In this generation, the political spirit, satisfied in pleasing man, will be allowed *by God* to rise into leadership positions—just as Saul was allowed by God to reign over His people for a season. Yet, during this political era, God found David soaking in the oil of intimacy with Him. It was in this place of intimacy where David was marked by God to be the leader of Israel. David's life of worship so moved the heart of God that He chose to bring His Son into this world through David's lineage.

In this hour there is a Davidic generation that has likewise devoted themselves to the place of worship and intimacy. It is an underground movement of worshipers that are fanning the flames of love and devotion to the Presence of God.

THE DAVIDIC GENERATION

When all was said and done, the religious ways of Saul and his political, man-pleasing regime were the vehicle that God used to shape His true leader. The Lord found David tucked away in the fields tending his father's sheep. David remained hidden, like an arrow in the quiver of the Lord, for years. Even after being anointed by Samuel as the next king, God walked him through a season of preparation.

The time came for David to come out of hiding in the secret place. God granted him a platform before the nation. 1 Samuel 17 is the well-known story when David slays Goliath. After this victory, David is brought into Saul's palace to serve under his leadership. I am sure that it must have been in the back of David's mind that this must be God's way of bringing His word to pass for David to become the next king. On top of that, David married Saul's daughter and became Saul's son-in-law; that much closer to the throne that he was destined for. Little did David know that he would soon be ducking spears being thrown at him from the hand of Saul himself and fleeing for his life.

From that time on David spent possibly some ten to twelve years running for his life (Scripture doesn't say how long). Saul diligently pursued after David with jealousy and murder in his heart. Twice David had the opportunity to slay Saul. Twice David refused to take matters into his own hands and strike down the anointed of the Lord. This is a man after God's own heart! The Lord found Him a man that would obey Him to completion. Though the enemy used Saul to attempt to kill David and his seed, God was able to use this evil and turn it around for His good. Saul's madness was the vehicle that would shape the character within David to be a true king to lead the people of God.

Through his life of worship, David was given access into the heart of God. He walked close enough to the heart of the Father to understand that, through his trials, God was shaping character within him. Even as Saul was chasing after him, David never dishonored him in his heart. He never slandered or cursed Saul. Nor did he wish for the day of his death. Never did he take matters into his own hands and attempt to overthrow this wicked regime.

This Davidic generation will walk with the same heart as David. What

David discovered in the secret place of worship we will find! The closer that we walk to the heart of God, the greater revelation we will have of the Father's heart. We will understand, like David, that the "Saul" leadership that currently reigns and the evil that corrupts the earth are only a vehicle to push us into the caves of intimacy with the Lord. The Lord is seeking worshipers, and more often than not, worshipers are birthed and matured through the furnace of affliction.

This Davidic generation will gain the attention of heaven through their lifestyle of abiding in the secret place. At the same time, they will also gain the jealous attention of the "Sauls" who are in leadership; but that's okay! What the devil means for our destruction, God, in His sovereignty, will turn it around and use it for His glory... just ask David!

If we had the opportunity to sit with David, I truly believe that he would tell us how thankful he was for what he learned through the affliction of being chased by Saul. Just read the book of Psalms! Many of the Psalms of David were written in the furnace of affliction and hiding in caves. As hard as it was on him, I'm sure he would tell us that he could not have become the king he was without the character that was developed through his trials.

The same will be true for this Davidic generation. When we look back at all the sufferings of this present time, they will not be able to be compared to the glory that shall be revealed through the trials that we have walked through. David constantly ran *into* the presence of God seeking refuge. Will we follow his example in this last hour? This is my question to this Davidic generation.

Next we will look into David's reign. His leadership established such a precedent that even Israel today looks for the Messiah to restore what David established three thousand years ago. Let's move past Saul into David's reign!

Chapter 9

LEGACY FOR ALL GENERATIONS

After this I will return and will rebuild the tabernacle of David which has fallen down; I will rebuild its ruins, and I will set it up; so that the rest of mankind may seek the Lord (Acts 15:16,17 NKJV).

In this hour it is in the heart of God to restore all things. In fact, restoration has always been in the heart of God. Yet Scripture is clear that the mystery of God has been hidden in His heart from the beginning and is only now being revealed. Peter tells us in Acts 3:21 that, *"He [Jesus] must remain in heaven until the time comes for God to restore everything, as He promised long ago through His holy prophets."*

In the early days of the church, the apostles lived and preached with an urgency that Christ was coming again within their generation. I do not believe that they had the knowledge that two thousand years later we would still be waiting upon His return—except perhaps John who was given the revelation. I do believe they had revelation that God would sum up all things within the time span of one generation. They lived with that urgency within their souls that time was short. As some of the churches were complaining about the Lord's delay, Peter admonished them saying:

But do not forget this one thing, dear friends: with the Lord a day is like a thousands years, and a thousand years are like a day. The

139

Lord is not slow in keeping his promise, as some understand slowness. Instead he is patient with you, not wanting anyone to perish, but everyone to come to repentance (2 Peter 3:8-9).

From the beginning, the Holy Spirit has always been the Faithful Witness. In the heart of God, His work is already completed and we are just walking out, in time, what has already been finished in the dwelling place of God. The Holy Spirit speaks through chosen vessels from the urgency of His completed work that is already summed up *in Him!* Let that blow your mind for a second. The Bible tells us that His chosen vessels are only able to grasp a part of what the Holy Spirit is speaking through them: *"For we know in part and we prophesy in part" (1 Corinthians 13:9).* Though the apostles were filled with the Spirit and were given revelation that has today become part of Holy Scripture, *they still only knew in part.*

All through the book of Acts we see a gradual unveiling of God's plan being wrought through His church. For a time, the apostles believed that the gospel was for the Jews only and that God's plan was to redeem Israel alone. So much so that the Holy Spirit had to send a vision to Peter to persuade him to go with the Roman soldiers to the house of Cornelius. Upon arriving at his house, God had to baptize them with the Holy Spirit with the evidence of speaking in tongues just so Peter would believe.

Though the early church was filled with the Spirit of God, they still had very limited knowledge of what was unveiling through their obedience to the Spirit. In Acts 13 the church at Antioch sent out Barnabas and Paul to do the work that the Lord had called them to accomplish. While on their mission for God, they continued to preach to the Jews that were dispersed into the nations. Finally, after much rejection by the Jewish people, Paul and Barnabas began preaching to the Gentiles. This became such an issue to the church at Jerusalem that they called for Paul and Barnabas to discuss this matter.

In Acts 15 we read about what has been called the "Jerusalem Council." This was a meeting of all the key leaders of the early church to fervently seek God to find out what His heart was saying about the Gentiles receiving the gospel. The early church fathers were under the belief that Christ was only sent to save Israel from their enemies and He was to reign over Israel from Jerusalem. This was partially correct; they just did not yet receive the revelation that God loved the whole world and Christ was sent to save all.

Upon diligently searching the Scriptures and seeking God, the apostles came to a conclusion. James, who is believed to be the leader of the church in Jerusalem, stood up and proclaimed:

Men and brethren, listen to me: Simon has declared how God at first visited the Gentiles to take out of them a people for His name. And with this the words of the prophets agree, just as it is written: "After this I will return and will rebuild the tabernacle of David, which has fallen down; I will rebuild its ruins, and I will set it up; so that the rest of mankind can seek the Lord ... Known to God from eternity are all His works" (Acts 15:13-18 NKJV).

The Holy Spirit opened the eyes of the early church and revealed His plan. For centuries, the Jews believed that the Messiah was coming to restore Israel to the glory that they had in the days of King David. This is absolutely true! Jesus will come and reign on the throne of David. This Scripture from Acts 15:16 was originally spoken by the prophet in Amos 9:11. The nation of Israel, under the rule of David, established such a glory that to this day the Jews look for Messiah to restore what they had in David's day. The Lord demonstrated His perfect love for all humanity by sending Christ into the world to first atone for all sins. It is not the Father's will that any should perish.

Christ *will* come a second time and restore all that was lost. He *will* reign on the throne of David, not just over Israel, but over all nations. So what is it about the reign of David that marked the heart of God? Let's look into this and gain revelation for this end time Davidic generation.

THE REIGN OF DAVID

In the last chapter, we took an in depth look into the life and reign of Saul. I now want us to move past his reign and look into the life of David. Both of these are great examples for us to learn from. What is it about David's life that God saw? Even as king, David committed sins that far outweighed Saul's simple acts of disobedience. So what is it that touched the Lord's heart even so much as to call David a man after His own heart?

David was a lover of the Presence of God even from the days of his youth. The Lord spoke to David through the prophet Nathan saying: *"I took you from the pasture and from following the flock to be ruler over My people Israel" (2 Samuel 7:8).* It also says in Psalm 78:70-72, *"He chose David His servant and took him from the sheep pens ... to be shepherd of His people Jacob ... And David shepherded them (Israel) with integrity of heart; with skillful hands he led them."* David captured the heart of the Lord in his early years simply because he was in love with His presence. When we keep in remembrance what Jesus said to the woman at the well; the Father found a worshiper in David! The Lord was not looking for a mighty warrior to lead Israel, He was looking for a lover of His presence.

The Lord has not changed His pursuit. He is still looking for a man or woman who is so in love with His Presence that nothing else matters. Have you ever been around someone who is in love? Oftentimes they are accused of having their head in the clouds because they can't stop thinking about the one they are in love with. I remember when I was courting my wife. I did some outright insane things to ensure that I would get to spend time with her. Then, when we got engaged, I counted the days and even the hours until the day of our wedding. It kept getting harder and harder to say goodbye every night because I was so in love. Even now that we are married, we are so in love that I have not missed one morning, before heading out the door, that I don't lean down while she is sleeping and tell her I love her and I can't wait to see her later. I do this because of love. I love how they say it at International House of Prayer in Kansas City: "Jesus is our magnificent obsession!" In much of society today, burning love could be considered obsessive. I have good news for many; *it's okay if you are obsessed with Jesus; it's called being in love!*

While the entire nation of Israel was under the heavy weight of war against the Philistines, David was out in the sheepfolds singing love songs to God on his harp. *This is what grabbed the heart of God!* The Lord does not need our strength in war or our skill with a sword. He does not need a man or woman well - educated in the Scriptures. Nor does He need our administrative skills or creative ideas for marketing. *What made David a man after God's own heart was his absolute dependence on the Presence of God; nothing more and nothing less!*

We read in Psalm 78:72 that David shepherded the people of God with integrity of heart and skillful hands. When taken into context with its frequent usage in the Psalms, it is used in relation to "playing skillfully on the instruments." Psalm 45 is called "a wedding song—a song of love" in which the writer speaks, *"My heart is stirred by a noble theme as I recite my verses for the king; my tongue is the pen of a SKILLFUL WRITER."* The "skill" that David led the people of God with was not his ability to slay giants (though he did). It was not his ability to slay his ten thousands while Saul only could slay his thousands. No, it was his skill and wisdom of keeping his heart in blazing love with the Presence of God all the days of his life; this is the life of a worshiper! David exudes a man who, through all the trials and all the victories, kept the flame of love burning until the end.

At the end of it all, it will only be those who stay in love with God that will truly endure this end time hour as antichrist takes his place. That is why Jesus could say about the last days, *"Because of the increase of wickedness, the love of most will grow cold, but he who stands firm to the end will be saved"* (Matthew 24:12). Who do you think Jesus is referring to when He talks about those standing firm till the end? He's talking about those whose love does not grow cold. *In other words, those who stay in love!*

This Davidic generation will capture what David caught in the secret place. His love and devotion to God was always his number one priority in life. Psalm 78:72 also speaks of the integrity of his heart. It is often said that integrity is what you do when nobody else is watching. You can easily translate that to what you do in secret. David's integrity or life in the secret place was fueled by a pure passion to please the Lord God of Israel. The Lord tested David on multiple occasions to reveal what was truly the motive of his heart. David could have twice taken Saul's life and his crown if that is what he was chasing after. Yet, because of his integrity, David's heart was convicted from the Lord in even stretching out his hand towards Saul.

David somehow found the purity of a Presence-driven life while he was young in the fields. Even while he was king you will see a constant pattern of David "inquiring of the Lord" before he did anything for God. Oh that this generation would have this heart after God that David carried within him! The Lord Himself could entrust the entire kingdom to a man who was in love with His Presence. The Lord knew that David would not fail Him:

> *I have found David son of Jesse a man after my own heart; he will do everything I want him to do ... Now when David had served God's purpose in his own generation, he fell asleep"* (Acts 13:22; 36).

The Lord also has a people in this generation who will serve His purpose like David!

During the reign of Saul, Scripture tells us that all the castaways and rejects of society flocked to David. *"All those who were in distress or in debt or discontented gathered around him [David], and he became their leader"* *(1 Samuel 22:2).* What an astounding man of God David was to turn a people who were the rejects of society into one of the greatest companies of mighty men that the earth has ever seen. What was it about David's leadership that took weak and defeated people and formed an unstoppable army? I believe it was his devotion to the Presence of God! I'm positive that these broken people paid close attention to David every time the journey got tough. Yet every time they watched David run into the Presence of God for refuge, I'm sure they followed right behind him. The king of their nation was chasing after their leader to kill him, but this company watched closely as David lived with integrity of heart—his skillful hands leading worship before their God.

Does this sound at all familiar? Does this not mirror the life of Jesus Himself? The Lord did not choose the nobles of society, but was accused of hanging out with the publicans and sinners. These rejects of Jesus' day are now the pillars upon which His kingdom stands. Jesus first brought His disciples to Himself before He ever sent them out into the world to do His work. This is the way of the Lord! He will not choose the mighty of this world to do His work lest the mighty boast of their strength. No, He is choosing the rejected of society and calling them first to come into His Presence. It is in His Presence where He defines us and heals all the wounds of rejection. From the place of obscurity, the Lord is raising up this Davidic generation to abide in His Presence. From the humble "sheepfolds" God is calling the weakest people and equipping them with nothing more than His Presence. He will not let the Sauls of this age put their armor on us. His Presence is all we need to be clothed with. We do not need a doctorate in divinity when God has already made us partakers of the divine nature through the blood of Jesus. For us to accomplish the will of the Father we only need His Presence!

Towards the end of David's reign, his son Absalom rose up against him and took his throne. Again David did not take matters into his own hands to fight against his son. He simply prayed and waited on God. He was such a man after God's own heart that when the priests were wanting to take the ark of God with his company, David refused. He loved the people and did not want the Presence for just himself. He told Zadok to *"Take the ark of God back into the city. If I find favor in the Lord's eyes, He will bring me back and let me see it and His dwelling place again"* (2 Samuel 15:25). David did not want the throne, he only wanted the Presence of God! The very essence of the kingdom of heaven is the Presence of the King. Heaven is only heaven because of His Presence. David understood this when his son stole the kingdom away. Israel belonged to God and His Presence is for all!

David carried a heart after God until the very end of his life; this is key! It is not he who starts on fire that God is after. It is those who stay on fire through it all that will change the earth. Staying on fire simply signifies staying in love. In the end, a worshiper is one who is in love with God. David was in love. Saul only disobeyed instruction and God stripped the kingdom away from him. David committed adultery with Bathsheba, killed her husband, then concealed the matter, yet God accepted his repentance. The difference between Saul and David is that David was in love with God, Saul was not. Saul was religious and tried with everything within in him to follow the way of the Lord; *but he was not in love!* His small failures ended in rejection because Saul was not in love, meaning his core motive was not to please God out of love. Saul wanted the blessing of God more than he wanted God Himself. David, on the other hand, sinned far worse than Saul but repented. David didn't care if he lost everything, he just wanted the Presence of God (see Psalm 51:11).

There is so much more that I could share about all that David did during his reign as king of Israel. What I really want us to understand is that it is not so much what David "did" that made him great but it's who David "was." He was a man after God's own heart. This is what made him great. The same is true for us today. What makes us a worshiper who pleases God is not in what we do as much as it is about who we are. When you are in love with God like David was, then everything you do is an outward reflection of who you are; a lover, a worshiper! This is what God is seeking; men and women *after, or in pursuit of,* His own heart.

THE KEY OF DAVID

There was a long season in my life, between 2007 through 2010, that God wrecked my life with the revelation of the power of a life devoted to worship and prayer. My life testimony is the story of one brought out of obscurity. I had no idea what God was doing through the 24-7 prayer movement until just a few years back. I really had no idea who was who in ministry or anything like that. In all honesty I thank God for this because I was introduced, in the secret place, to the 24-7 prayer and worship that has been taking place around His throne forever. 24-7 worship and prayer is not just a new trendy thing in the church culture. It's what has always been taking place around the throne and always will be. Worship is the response of creation to the Presence of the Creator. I have news for you all; God is always going to be around so worship will never cease!

During the spring of 2010, the Lord called me to a forty-day period of fasting and prayer. In our small two-bedroom apartment, my wife and I turned our second bedroom into a prayer room. We had an ipod that was constantly playing worship music. During this forty-day period, I would set my alarm for midnight and get up and pray for an hour. I must be honest with you, oftentimes I would pray in tongues for ten minutes then wake up an hour later, but God saw my sincere heart to seek His face.

There was one night in particular that I remember like yesterday. The spirit of intercession hit me like fire and I began groaning with the groans of heaven. I was crying out for my city saying: "God, please send fire into our city; God, send revival, send revival!" I remember lifting up my Bible before the Lord asking, "Why are we not seeing a move of God like this Bible tells us about, Lord? God, send revival like the apostles saw in the book of Acts!" By this time I was weeping profusely while lying on my face. I repeatedly said: "God, give us the keys, God, give us the keys." I repeated this until I had no more strength and I lay there weeping until I had no more tears. Then, almost like a blanket of perfect peace, the glory of God came into my room. I heard the Lord say into my spirit these words, "*The Key of David ...The Key of David.*" At this, He had my attention! He then said to me, "*The Key of David was given to the church in Philadelphia*" (see Revelation 3). He then asked me, "*What does Philadelphia mean?*" I knew the answer so I said out loud, "the city of brotherly love." The Lord then said something to me that has changed my life to this day. He said, "*It is not until My people come together and gather around My Presence that I will pour out this end time revival that you are asking for. I will not pour out My Spirit over any one church, ministry, or denomination. I will pour out My Spirit over cities and nations.*"

The Lord then opened my eyes to see that He does not reduce the Body of Christ to anything smaller than a city. He does not separate the churches like we separate. Even the epistles in the New Testament are written to the church in "Rome, Corinth, Ephesus, etc." For those of you that don't know, these names are cities in the days of the early church. He then said to me: "*The Key of David opens doors that no man can close and it closes doors that no man can reopen. The Key of David is worship and intimacy with Me! Worship and intimacy opens the everlasting doors for the King of Glory to come into cities. This is the key that David had!*" It was in that moment that my life was changed forever. I devoted my life to the secret place of worship and prayer. In that moment, I gave myself to His burning Presence to contend for my city.

During the season leading up to this encounter with God, the Lord was strongly dealing with me about the motives behind everything that I was doing for Him. Everything that was not motivated by His selfless love He exposed in me. I would hear the Lord whisper into my ear during prayer: "selfish ambitions." I knew He was speaking about me and exposing the motives of my heart. At that time, I was also going through Bible college with what I thought were sincere motives to serve Him. Yet my "selfish ambition" was to climb the ladder of success and build a ministry, eventually preach on large platforms, and in all honesty, become a popular minister. I mean, isn't that what our culture teaches us? In my "selfish ambition" I was deceiving myself into believing that I was doing it all for His kingdom. It was during this season of consecration that God was setting me apart for what He has called us all to; Himself not ministry.

There were two other vehicles that God used during this time to mark my soul forever. The first one was a song by Jason Upton called "Dying Star." This is a powerful song where God is singing over Jason about the danger of the pride within us all. He sang of the ministries that are rising like "stars." Because of this, the whole world is now staring at them and they cannot see God. The end result of these "stars" is the same that we have seen in church history; they fall and become just another dying star. I would listen to this over and over again and just weep like a baby.

The other tool that God used was a sermon called "A Generation of Its" by a man of God named Damon Thompson. This message marked my soul. He preached about a generation that God is raising up that doesn't want to become a "who" but is willing to become an "it." A generation that doesn't want to become a "name" but will become a "voice in the wilderness" like John the Baptist. He even mentioned the song by Jason Upton that was already marking me. Damon summed up this message by saying that God is raising up "blacksmiths." In the days of Saul, the Philistines removed the blacksmiths from the land. Though Israel had a king and a prophet, the enemy was not afraid because there were no blacksmiths. Blacksmiths are the ones who will sit in a dark, fiery place and pound on metal to make weapons to put into soldiers hands so that others can fight.

The life of a blacksmith is a life devoted to the secret place that will never be seen on platforms, but their job is key to victory for the kingdom.

These two messages, along with other key events, are the vehicles that God used to prepare my heart for that night in the spring of 2010. Ever since God revealed to me the revelation of the "Key of David" I have devoted myself to hiding in His Presence and searching out the secret behind turning that key to unlock the everlasting doors through worship. Every ambition and dream for success, even in ministry, is now on the altar of worship before the Lord. Like Abraham, God asked me to put my dreams on His altar and be willing to put to death my future to fulfill His dream over a generation. Let us all put to death our own dreams and follow *His* dream over our cities and nations. This is the Key of David! His aspirations were never to be king, only to abide in the Presence of the Lord all the days of his life (see Psalm 27:4).

Worship is the key that will unlock the everlasting gates over our cities and nations; this is the key to the house of David. The day when the Body of Christ will throw aside every ambition for "self" promotion and put absolute priority on the Presence of God is the day we will see cities and nations turn to God. We have so many good ideas, and we are so busy trying to do all the right things. Yet I believe what we are lacking is a generation who is IN LOVE! We know how to do church. We know how to build beautiful buildings. We know how to pay all the bills. My question for you is this: *do we know how to fan the flame of love?* If God took away all the comforts of the modern day church; the comfortable seats, air-conditioned buildings, and powerful sound systems; if He stripped all those comforts away, would we still have mega-churches packed out? *Would we still maintain our burning hearts?*

Have we tried so hard to reach people for God that we have forfeited His Presence in doing so? Have we left our first love in pursuit of doing ministry? What God revealed to me that night in the spring of 2010 has never left my heart. It is not until we, as the Body of Christ in cities, put aside every other pursuit but burning for His Presence that His dream will be fulfilled. His dream is to cover the earth with the glory of the Lord as the waters cover the sea (see Habakkuk 2:14). This is the Key of David that will unlock the everlasting doors over our cities.

The life of David is full of so much revelation and insight that cannot be exhausted; from his childhood of tending sheep in the fields of obscurity, to his days of running from Saul and hiding in caves, all the way through his forty years as king. His whole life is packed with prophetic insight for this end time generation. Yet, I believe his greatest accomplishment in life is one that much of the Body of Christ as a whole knows very little about. It is called "The tabernacle of David."

THE TABERNACLE OF DAVID

During the council at Jerusalem in Acts 15, James alludes to a passage from Amos 9:11: *"After this I will return and will rebuild the tabernacle of David which has fallen down: I will rebuild its ruins."* How many of us just pass by that Scripture? I know I did for many years, never knowing what the tabernacle of David was, and I never really paid it a second thought. Yet, I believe for us to really get a full grasp on the heart of David, we must learn what this tabernacle was and why the Lord said, through Amos, that He was going to rebuild this tabernacle in the last days.

After the death of Saul, David reigned for seven years in Hebron, mostly over the tribe of Judah. Toward the end of this seven-year period, the entire nation of Israel began to flock to David and submit themselves willingly under his leadership. In this time, David perceived that it was the Lord who was transitioning the entire kingdom under his rule. He did not have to go, by force, to bring the nation under submission to his leadership.

As his first official act as king over the entire nation from Jerusalem, David assembled all the elders and the commanders of his army. In this gathering, David does not get up and say: "Now that I'm your king we are going to go and fight the Philistines and all the Lord's enemies!" No, David does not get up with war in his heart. What he does do is demonstrate the true passion of his heart: *"Let us bring the ark of our God back to us, for we did not inquire of it during the reign of Saul" (1 Chronicles 13:3).*

LEGACY FOR ALL GENERATIONS

Let us see this heart that David had! Nothing else mattered to him but the Presence of God. The ark represents the Presence and it was His Presence that David went after as his first official act as king. What leadership! David gathered all the warriors, who had been trained to have war in their hearts, and he demonstrated a man after God's own heart. His first act as king of Israel was to go and bring back God's Presence and to institute worship in the midst of the nation; the entire nation agreed! Can you imagine for one minute what would happen in America if our president got up as his first act as leader and called for all to worship Jesus? This is exactly what David did as king. He did this because it was the passion of his heart. David lived always in pursuit of the Presence of God. Jesus said: *"Out of the abundance of the heart the mouth speaks"* and *"You will know a tree by its fruit."* In other words, who we are at the center of our being is seen in our action. The heart represents the center, or core, of who we are. The very heart of David was worship! As I stated earlier, worship is not what we do, it's who we are; yet a worshiper will act out their inward desire to show their love for God.

David, along with the entire assembly of Israel, went to Kiriath Jearim where the ark was kept in the house of Abinadab. They built a brand new cart to carry the ark and they departed for Jerusalem. David and all of Israel worshiped the Lord with all their might as they traveled with the Presence of God in their midst. As they came to the threshing floor of Kidon, the oxen stumbled, and the ark began to fall from the cart. Uzzah reached out his hand to steady the ark and he died right there. At this the worship service stopped and, in all honesty, scared the daylights out of everybody, including David.

My question for you is this: Why is it significant that Uzzah died attempting to steady the ark? Why is this important enough to be placed in Holy Scripture? According to the Law of Moses, the ark was to be carried on the shoulders of the Levite priests. This is extremely significant to us because this tells us prophetically that the Presence of God is to be carried on the shoulders of priests! Revelation 1:6 tells us that Christ has made us all to be a "kingdom of priests unto His Father!" We are all created to carry the Presence of God upon us and within us.

After three months of the ark being housed with Obed Edom, David again rallies the nation to go and bring it into Jerusalem. This time he did his homework and appointed priests to carry the ark. With great celebration and praise, the ark is brought into Jerusalem and set on what would later be called Mount Zion. It was placed underneath a tent that would become known as the tabernacle of David. Other modern translations also refer to this as the tent of David as well.

This tent or tabernacle that David pitched was a simple structure where the ark was visibly seen on the top of Mount Zion. Now, what we must understand is that God Himself ordained through Moses that the ark was to be kept behind the veil in the tabernacle of Moses. Only once a year, on the Day of Atonement, was the High Priest allowed to come into His Presence. So what David did was absolutely against the law! Why was David allowed to live? We have seen what happened to Saul when he just tried to offer a sacrifice to God—he was rebuked by Samuel because it was not for kings to offer the sacrifices. His disobedience cost him the kingdom. Yet David is allowed to take the ark out of the prescribed tabernacle of Moses and pitch a simple tent? Scripture even tells us that David wore a linen ephod, which was only to be worn by priests who ministered to the Lord. How can this be? I'll tell you why; *it was David's heart! His passionate love broke through the barriers of the Law even before the age of grace that Jesus bought through His blood!* I will return to this thought later.

In the book of 1 Chronicles 15-17 we see an amazing account of the establishment of the tabernacle that David pitched for the Presence of God. David hired four thousand to minister before the Lord; two hundred eighty-eight were prophetic singers (see 1 Chronicles 23:4; 25:8). *"They were to play the lyres and harps, Asaph was to sound the cymbals, and Benaiah and Jahaziel the priests were to blow the trumpets regularly before the ark of the covenant" (1 Chronicles 16:4-6).* What David established here with the tabernacle of David is historic: four thousand musicians taking turns night and day in worship to the Lord. Twenty-four hours a day, seven days a week, David instituted worship to be in Israel. This got the attention of God so much that He prophesied, through Amos, that He would rebuild this tabernacle that David built for Him.

Some question whether or not David instituted praise and worship that continued 24-7. This is argued by interpreting "day and night" as only twice a day worship services much like the sacrifices that were to be offered once in the morning and once in the evening in the tabernacle of Moses. This is a valid argument. Yet, the key to it all is the word "regularly". The Hebrew word here is "tamiyd" which signifies "duration, continuance, perpetually, daily (both morning and evening, day and night) always and at all times; without interruption!" [1] This Hebrew word is very rich and signifies more than a casual continuance. In fact, it was most frequently used in reference to the sacrifices that were to be offered continually before the Lord and the fire that was to be continually burning before Him.

What David captured in his early days as a shepherd boy, as he sang love songs to the Lord, never left his heart as king of Israel. The tabernacle of David became an outward expression of his heart that was so in love with God that 24-7 worship and prayer was all that David could give back to God. Time could not contain the flame of love that was burning within him. The tabernacle of David becomes an Old Testament picture of a New Testament reality where there is no longer need for blood sacrifices to atone for sin according to the Law of Moses. Instead, we bring the simplicity of a burning heart that is in love with the Lord with sacrifices of praise and offering ourselves on the altars. With such praises God is pleased to inhabit and to even sit enthroned upon. This is the true priestly ministry that we have been ordained into; praise and worship that God Himself can reign through! This is what David caught in the secret place.

David caught a glimpse of what is happening around the throne of God in heaven; a nonstop worship gathering with seraphim and cherubim, twenty-four elders and an innumerable host of angels. David did all he could to bring the kingdom of heaven onto the earth; he instituted 24-7 worship and prayer in Israel. He reigned in Jerusalem for thirty-three years as king and his first act as king was to institute 24-7 worship, which consisted of four thousand skilled musicians. From this place, most of the book of Psalms came forth from the prophetic psalmists prophesying on their instruments. Many of these Psalms are prophecies that are

THE END TIME WORSHIP ARMY

still coming to pass even today. For thirty-three years the tabernacle of David remained in Jerusalem. Do you know where else in Scripture we see thirty-three years? You guessed it; the life of Jesus, the Son of David!

I believe the tabernacle of David is the greatest Old Testament picture of the New Testament church; the tabernacle not made with human hands. This is why I believe that the Lord refused David's request to build Him a temple on earth. The tabernacle that David pitched for the Lord on Mount Zion already captured the heart of God and He was pleased to inhabit the praises of His worshipers! David pulled His Presence out of the four wall boundaries prescribed by the Law of Moses and God's plan was not for him to build a temple made by human hands. David's tabernacle foreshadowed the New Testament Body of Christ and His dwelling place; the hearts of His worshipers! Even when Nathan prophesied to David that his son would be the one to build the house of the Lord, He was not talking about Solomon building the Temple; *He was* prophesying of *the Son of God Jesus Christ that would build His church that the gates of hell would not prevail against!*

For thirty-three years the tabernacle of David hosted the Presence of God on Mount Zion. For thirty-three years the Son of David Jesus Christ fulfilled the prophecy and became the True Tabernacle of God that He was pleased to dwell within. This is the tabernacle of David that He will build again in the last days. We are once again beginning to see 24-7 houses of prayer that are emerging out of the ashes of dead religion. Burning hearts are again capturing the vision that David caught to keep the fire of worship burning continually. The heart of David was not so much to wear out the people of God by attempting to push them to worship and pray all the time, but it was about keeping the Presence of God priority. On the earth today, the houses of prayer and burn furnaces that are emerging are not fueled by a works-driven religious heart to force people to earn God's love. No! They are fueled by the same heart that David carried within him that found a resting place in the flame of perfect love. As human beings we are bound by time so 24-7 is the most we can give, and still it is not enough to satisfy the longing inside of our burning hearts. Our lives become the tabernacle of David that God Himself inhabits through a lifestyle of 24-7 burning love.

This Davidic generation is fueled by the same fire of love that David had. The Presence of God is all we desire. Church does not cut it if God is not there. If we must wander into the wilderness of fasting and the caves of intimacy and prayer then that is what we must do. David was a man that could break the Law because he was in love. The boundaries of religion were not his boundaries and neither will religion dictate to this generation that we can only go so far. This Davidic generation will make the religious angry with their exuberant worship and crazy faith that sometimes break rules to press into His Presence. Just like in the days of Jesus, crazy faith, which worked through love, broke through the religious rules and touched His Presence. This is the Davidic generation!

Chapter 10

THE BURNING ONES

In the year that King Uzziah died, I saw the Lord seated on a throne, high and exalted, and the train of His robe filled the temple. Above Him were seraphim ... and they were calling to one another "Holy, Holy, Holy is the Lord Almighty; the whole earth is full of His glory" (Isaiah 6:1-3 NIV).

In the last chapter, I discussed a night in the spring of 2010 that God marked me in the secret place with revelation into the Key of David. For the next couple of months following that night, He continued to reveal Himself to me in ways that have changed me forever. 2 Corinthians 3:18 says,

But we all, with unveiled face, beholding as in a mirror the glory of the Lord, are being transformed into the same image from glory to glory, just as by the Spirit of the Lord (NKJV).

It is only as we behold Him, by revelation, that we are transformed into that same image. I like to say it this way: *You become what you behold.* During this season of consecration, the place of worship became my refuge of beholding His beauty. In this place of beholding, God has transformed me and marked my soul with His image and He continues to do so as I abide on my face before Him.

During that summer of 2010, the Lord brought me through another defining season of revolutionizing my secret place. This all happened leading up to Labor Day weekend in early September and theCall Sacramento. TheCall was the defining moment for my wife and me, and was key to launching us into our ministry with the Burn 24-7 and other relationships that we value to this day.

I remember getting together with some of our friends, and God would literally fall into our fellowship time and His fire would ignite in our midst. The Lord would speak through us fresh revelation of His heart and we would end up turning many of these times into prayer meetings. This became such a regular occurrence that we began to say to each other, "Let's get together and BURN again!" We even started joking around and calling each other "Burning Ones" because of the fire that we felt for even hours after hanging out together.

That whole summer leading up to theCall, the Lord began speaking into my spirit regularly saying: *"I am raising up a generation of Burning Ones. Those whose sole desire is to burn in My Presence. From this place of burning I will release My Presence into the earth."* I was able to slightly comprehend what He was saying to me because I was currently living in that reality of spending time with "Burning Ones." The Lord will often times speak to us right where we are at. Having no idea that God was about to connect us with "The Burn" ministry, God prepared us by putting language into what He was about to do. I love what my former pastor used to say: "The Lord is preparing us for what He already has prepared for us." I understood what He was saying to me based on what was happening when we gathered with our friends. Our God is a consuming fire; and when we gather in His Presence, we will also catch on fire!

Anytime I hear the Lord speak to me in this way I set myself to seek the Scripture to verify and solidify what He is saying. Proverbs 25:2 says, *"It is the glory of God to conceal a matter, but the glory of kings is to search a matter out"* (NKJV). In other words, when the Lord speaks, there are endless treasures of revelation that He will only uncover to a seeking heart.

When God speaks by His Spirit, and we catch the breath of His Word, it is very important that we find biblical language to communicate what God is saying. Not to bind or control the move of the Spirit, but to simply build each other up in faith and to have a firm biblical foundation to stand upon.

Even in the days of the early church the apostles devoted themselves to building a scriptural foundation to define what God was pouring out through His Spirit. For example, on the day of Pentecost, when tongues of fire fell upon the disciples and they all spoke with tongues, revival hit Jerusalem! Peter didn't look at everybody and say, "This is the new move of God and if you don't like it, get over it!." No, he got up and did everything he could to put scriptural language to the situation by saying, *This is what was spoken by the Prophet Joel" (Acts 2:16).* This is a constant pattern through Acts. The apostles were not being critical or religious; they were walking in wisdom and love for the people of God by following the move of the Spirit with scriptural definition.

The same is true for us in this last hour. God is pouring out His Spirit in even greater measures than the book of Acts. Yet it is up to us as His people to put biblical language to what is happening. In doing so, this will help us to faithfully steward what God is pouring out. This is why I believe Jesus says to all seven churches in the book of Revelation, *"He who has an ear to hear, let him hear what the Spirit is saying to the churches."* I say this because I believe it is our glory, as kings and priests of God, to establish through Scripture what God is saying through His Spirit in this last hour. God spoke to me for months that He is raising up a "generation of Burning Ones", yet I did not just stop there and say, "Okay God." Since then I have diligently sought who these "Burning Ones" are and what treasures can I find in Scripture to add more to what God has revealed! Now I have the honor of sharing my findings with you. You all have a place in the midst of this generation of Burning Ones!

THE SERAPHIM

In Isaiah, Chapter 6, the Lord gives to His prophet a vision that very much mirrors the vision of John in the book of Revelation, Chapters 4 and 5.

This Scripture has become a breeding ground of revelation that has fueled my pursuit with even greater passion to know the Lord more. He says,

> *In the year that King Uzziah died, I saw the Lord, high and exalted, seated on a throne, and the train of His robe filled the temple. Above Him were seraphim, each with six wings: with two wings they covered their faces, with two they covered their feet, and with two they were flying. And they were calling to one another: "Holy, Holy, Holy is the Lord Almighty; the whole earth is full of His glory" (vv. 1-3).*

In this vision, Isaiah gives a specific description of angelic beings that he calls "seraphim"—these angelic beings surround the throne of God. The literal translation from this Hebrew word is "on fire ones, burning ones or even more literally: fiery flying serpents."[1] These angelic seraphim dwell so close to the Presence of God that they are *burning!* They have the name in heaven as being on fire. I love it! No other being in heaven has been given such a name as the seraphim or "Burning Ones"

The seraphim are not to be mistaken with the cherubim that also have a place around the throne of God. Both Ezekiel and John speak of "living creatures" in visions that God gave to them. Ezekiel testifies that these living creatures seem almost to be carriers of the Presence of God (see Ezekiel 1). Later, in Ezekiel 10, he reveals these living creatures by name as cherubim. These can also describe the living creatures that the apostle John saw in Revelation 4 and 5 encircling the throne. The cherubim are also seen in Genesis 3 being given the assignment to guard the way of the Tree of Life. We also see the cherubim engraved into the veil of the temple leading into the most holy place. These cherubim even stand on both sides of the mercy seat within the veil. Through multiple Scriptures, the cherubim are believed to have the assignment as guardians and protectors of the holiness of God's Presence.

So who are these seraphim? They are crying out the same words as the four living creatures (or cherubim) in Revelation 4 and 5. So why are they given a distinct name in heaven as the "burning ones"? I believe one of the keys to this is found in verse 2 *"Above Him were seraphim."* Above

Him? Above God? I have at times pondered if this is a misprint, but it's not; every translation says the same. Where else in Scripture will you ever see anything or anyone above God? There is no other being that you will see "above" God except the seraphim. Now, before I go any further, let me say quickly that our God is the Most High! There is none above Him in the place of power or authority, but I will tell you that He humbles Himself and even made Himself of no reputation and became obedient to death on the Cross (see Phiippians 2:7-9).

I believe the seraphim become a picture to us of the worshipers that God inhabits. He chooses to humble Himself to be lifted up in their praise. God gives place to these "Burning Ones" to be exalted in their worship. Like David, these burning ones are worshipers by nature. Created to worship, these burning ones abide so close to the Presence of God that the fire of His holiness consumes them. They have such a place in heaven, above the throne, that God is lifted up in their worship.

"AT THE SOUND OF THEIR VOICES"

The Lord is raising up a generation of Burning Ones in this hour. These "burning ones" or seraphim, I believe, reveal to us the absolute picture of the power of worship and the place of His worshipers in heaven. Isaiah 6 gives us such a distinct look into the worship that takes place around the throne of God: *"At the sound of their voices the doorposts and thresholds shook and the temple was filled with smoke." v. 4).* Now, it took me quite a few times of reading this over to get this! It does not say, "At the sound of God's voice"; I can see His voice shaking heaven. It doesn't say that it is the voice of God, it says: *"At the sound of THEIR voices..."* It is their worship that shakes the foundations of heaven!

I have said this before and I say again: True worship is the response of the created being to the revelation of the Creator. These burning ones in heaven are gazing into the glory of God and crying, *"Holy, Holy, Holy is the Lord Almighty; the whole earth is filled with His glory."* These burning ones are not just singing some song like we have turned this into; *they are responding to what they see!* The very response of their inward being is crying out and their cry is shaking the doorposts of heaven. This is worship! Their worship fills the temple in heaven with smoke.

In ancient Hebrew writing, when any word was emphasized, they would write it out twice, much like how in English literature, we use exclamation points. Hebrew writers would express exclamation by writing a word twice. To stress exclamation to the highest degree, the Hebrew writers would write the word three times. This was a very rare occasion, but it stressed to the highest degree what was being expressed. So what Isaiah most likely heard was not the seraphim simply saying 'holy' three different times in a humble tone, but an absolute outburst from these angels, exploding from within, crying out one word "HOLY!" So much so that he could only describe what he heard to the third degree of expression. Imagine for one moment these burning angels gazing into our God, who is a consuming fire. One gaze into His infinite glory results in an explosion of worship that shakes the foundation of heaven. *This is worship!* This is what happens when true worship breaks out! This is the power of a worshiping army. God is raising up a generation of Burning Ones in this hour that are gazing at God in His glory and their worship is shaking the foundations of heaven.

"IN THE YEAR THAT KING UZZIAH DIED"

Some of you might be asking: "What does this have to do with the end times?" This was also my question as well until God began to open my eyes. Isaiah begins this vision by saying: *"In the year that King Uzziah died..."* I have heard different interpretations from others about what this means, but I began to seek God about this for myself. I am not saying that the other revelations of this Scripture are wrong; all that I have heard has been amazing and edifying. Yet sometimes we just have to go after God for personal revelation. This is what the Lord showed to me about this Scripture.

King Uzziah brought the kingdom of Judah to one of their most prosperous hours since the early days of Solomon when the kingdom was not divided between Judah and Israel. His fame spread abroad and the army

THE BURNING ONES

of Judah was strengthened and unstoppable all the while Uzziah sought the Lord. Judah never reached such a plateau of success as they did under the rule of Uzziah. Yet at the end of his reign, he was lifted up in pride and fell from his kingship; even so much that the Lord struck Uzziah with leprosy and he was cast out from the presence of His people. So the year of his death was a very grievous time in the history of Judah. Yet it was in this hour that the Lord chose to lift Isaiah up into the Spirit to show him heaven's perspective.

In a very dark hour for Judah, God takes Isaiah up into the Spirit and releases revelation of throne room worship. He sees these Burning Ones crying out and declaring the holiness of God and decreeing that the earth is full of His glory. Let me ask you something: was the earth filled with His glory? Is it now, some 2700 years later? The answer, of course, is no. Not from human perspective anyway. Even Isaiah's response reveals this: "*Woe is me! ...I am ruined! For I am a man of unclean lips, and I live among a people of unclean lips, and my eyes have seen the King, the Lord Almighty.*" In the Presence of God, Isaiah became undone, yet the seraphim are declaring and prophesying glory into the earth through their worship.

No matter how dark the hour in history, in the Presence of God is fullness of joy! In Him all things have been summed up and His work is complete. He is King forever and in His Presence we rest in that hope. The Burning Ones were not too concerned about how dark the hour was in the year that King Uzziah died. Neither were they concerned through all the darkest hours of history. They also are not shaken by the rise of antichrist in this last hour. In fact, it is as they respond to the Presence of God in worship that their voices create such a shaking in heaven that the smoke of God's glory fills the temple. Much like in the days of Solomon when the temple was completed, he called for the worshipers and musicians:

All the Levites who were musicians ... stood on the east side of the altar, dressed in fine linen and playing cymbals, harps and lyres. They were accompanied by 120 priests sounding trumpets. The trumpeters and singers joined in unison, as with one voice, to give praise and thanks to the Lord ... Then the temple of the Lord was filled with a cloud, and the priests could not perform their service because of the cloud, for the glory of the Lord filled the temple (2 Chronicles 5:12-14).

Do you see the correlation here between the Burning Ones in heaven and the true worshipers here on earth? God inhabits exuberant praise, then worship breaks out when God shows up! This response to God releases a shaking that then releases greater glory into the earth. We see this also in the book of Revelation, Chapter 8. The apostle John records in his vision:

When He opened the seventh seal, there was silence in heaven for about half an hour. And I saw the seven angels who stand before God, and to them were given seven trumpets. Then another angel, having a golden censer, came and stood at the altar. He was given much incense, that he should offer it with the prayers of the saints upon the golden altar which was before the throne. And the smoke of the incense, with the prayers of the saints, ascended before God from the angel's hand. Then the angel took the censer, filled it with fire from the altar, and threw it to the earth. And there were noises, thunderings, lightnings, and an earthquake (Revelation 8:1-5 NKJV).

We plainly see this same smoke that Isaiah saw rising before the Lord in the end times that produces a shaking in the earth that ushers in the final judgments that prepare the world for the second coming of Jesus.

This is what God was saying to me, by His Spirit, before I ever understood this. "From this place of burning I will release My Presence into the Earth." I hope you understand now why I stated how important it is to bring scriptural language to what the Spirit is saying and doing. True worship comes forth from the place of revelation! These Burning Ones are gazing into God, and worship is breaking out from within the very fiber of their being. As God unveils another facet of His glory that they have yet to see, worship breaks out! The sound of their worship releases greater glory as heaven shakes. This is what God is raising up in this hour with the true worshipers. At the sound of their voices the gates of heaven will open up and the King of Glory will come into His house with greater revelation of the beauty of His holiness.

"HE TOUCHED MY MOUTH"

"Then one of the seraphim flew to me with a live coal in his hand, which he had taken with tongs from the altar. With it he touched my mouth and said, 'See, this has touched your lips; your guilt is taken away and your sin is atoned for" (vv. 6-7)

After all of this intense worship that brought Isaiah to a revelation of His lack of personal holiness and a need for more of God, one of these seraphim touched the lips of this prophet with fire from the altar. As I have said before, I say again: *there is an absolute need for the fire of God in this hour!* This generation is being touched by the fire of God. Even more, *they will stay on fire and burn;* this is the generation of Burning Ones. If we are called to abide in God, then we are called to abide in His fire. He is fire, and to be in Him is to be on fire.

One important thing that we must know about fire is the cleansing that comes through burning. For any individual who wants to hold on to sin, then the fire of God will torment them, but the one who falls in love, this same fire that torments others becomes the passion that fuels deeper love for God. It is the flame of His Presence that separates everything within us that keeps us from drawing closer to Him. You see this very clearly with Isaiah. When he came close to the fire, all he could do was complain about the sin within him and the sins of those around him. He was consumed with the conditions on the earth in which he dwelt. Yet the seraphim were not giving a second thought to what was happening in the earth. They were consumed with the Presence of God and declaring prophecy over the earth. In this moment the seraphim were sent from the altar to touch the lips of Isaiah with fire. They declared over him that his guilt was taken away and his sin was atoned for.

I would like to take a little more time with this. What is being said here? Why is it important that his guilt be taken away and that his sin be atoned for? Was he not already a prophet called by God? What does this mean for us today? It means everything for us. I have said this before: *the root of sin is self!* In other words, for us to have our sin atoned for, plus the guilt and shame removed, we don't just need forgiveness from our acts of sin. What needs to be removed is the root of sin which is self; the self centered nature of sin that we are all born into.

When Isaiah came into the glory of God in all His fullness, the only thing that he could do was turn inward. Yet the will of God is not for us to turn inward but for us to get our eyes off ourselves and see Him. When this happens, then His fire will purge our selfish nature and we will see Him with greater clarity. It is from the place of clearly beholding Him that we can prophesy from the place of revelation and promise—not discouragement, death, and despair.

Let us get this! In this last hour there is an unleashing of great evil into the earth. As the antichrist spirit continues to push God and His Son Jesus out of society, the increase of wickedness will continue to rise. Jesus tells us *"Because of the increase of wickedness, the love of most shall grow cold"* *(Matthew 24:12 KJV).* This generation cannot afford to be distracted with the rise of wickedness as it abounds in the earth. This is what happened with Isaiah; he was consumed with the sin that was around him. This also can happen to us when we remain sin-focused and not God-focused. Sin must be addressed, but not at the expense of becoming a focal point that steals the attention of our beautiful God. Sin has been dealt with at the Cross, and when we get our eyes off of our own sin (self) then we will see Him clearly. What once had our attention only fades away in the beauty of His holiness.

In this hour, this generation of Burning Ones will overcome the spirit of religious condemnation that drags many down. Though the increase of wickedness will abound in the land, these Burning Ones will have their consciences cleansed and their selfish ways atoned for through the fire of His Presence. When we live our lives constantly fixated on sin and evil, then we will constantly live under the weight of condemnation. This spirit carries with it a false humility of always "feeling" unworthy and unable to

THE BURNING ONES

live a life that God is pleased with. This is what happened to Isaiah when he came into the Presence of the holy fire of God, and this is what happens to us all. We have all sinned and fallen short of the glory of God.

The Burning Ones in this generation will live constantly fixated on God and the beauty of His holiness. We must redeem holiness from the ugly, legalistic word that religion has painted for the bride of Christ. We worship in "the beauty of holiness." Holiness is beautiful when sin is no longer our focus. When we take our eyes off of ourselves and *our eyes have seen the King*" then fire will touch our lips and our confession will no longer be complaints about the conditions around us. Our God is burning with passion to redeem the earth. His will is to prepare a bride for His Son; Holy is our God! Holiness is not seen by the works of God, it is who God is! He is completely separate from His creation, and we are holy because He is holy. Yes, in His Presence, God convicts us of sin, for all have sinned. God has already condemned the sinful, self-centered nature within us and He releases grace to those who simply respond to His conviction and humble themselves before His throne. This is how Paul could say: *"There is therefore now no condemnation for those who are in Christ Jesus, who do not walk according to the flesh* [selfish, sin nature], *but according to the Spirit" (Romans 8:1 NKJV).*

The seraphim look into the Presence of God, who is a consuming fire, and they cry out "holy"! Their response to the Presence of God shakes the doorposts or gates of heaven and releases greater glory into the temple. Isaiah, on the other hand, sees nothing but his own sin and the sin around him and all he can say is "woe is me, woe is me. I am unclean." The devil's scheme is to get us to keep our eyes focused on ourselves and our inward issues. While we sit around attempting, year after year, to get our lives right in our own eyes, we have rendered the kingdom within us ineffective. Our confession will never change from complaining and saying, "Woe is me...Woe is me" to "Holy is the Lord! The Earth is full of His glory." As long as we make this about us, then God is not glorified. It is not who we are that will change the earth, it's who He is! Worship is all about Him. This is the scheme of the enemy and the goal of dead religion to render an entire generation ineffective; *but not this generation!*

In this last hour, God is raising up Burning Ones who have seen the King in all His glory. They are not going to let dead religion hold them back from approaching the throne of God and living in the fire of His holiness. These fiery worshipers will not be held down by the evil that is gathering to fight against the Lord and His Christ. They will gaze into God and stay in love! Even as the pain of burning in His fire devours all that offends God is burned away, these Burning Ones will endure the process of being purified because they will remain in love. From this place of burning passion and love, the Presence of God will flow through them and release fire into the earth. Their worship will move the heavens and shake the earth.

No matter how dark the hour gets, these Burning Ones will be a bright and burning lamp where the broken and outcasts of this world will find refuge in their light. Much like John the Baptist, you will not find these Burning Ones in king's palaces or dressed in fine raiment. You will find them in the wilderness crying out to their generation to come back to their first love before the door is finally shut. At the sound of their voices the everlasting gates are opening up and the King of Glory is about to come and sit on His throne. The fire of God is consuming this generation and producing worship that moves God on behalf of His bride. Jump into the fire and become a Burning One, you will never be the same!

Chapter 11

THE BELOVED BRIDE

"I am my beloved's, and my beloved is mine"
(Song of Solomon 6:3 KJV).

It is innate within the fallen nature of man to find their identity in what they do; especially in this capitalistic western society. The slogan for the culture in which we live is, "Everyone has the right to the pursuit of their own happiness." This is the American dream, am I right? Because of this, many give themselves to their careers in pursuit of fulfilling their dream to be successful. The problem with this is the emptiness that the human soul is left with at the end of this pursuit. Families have fallen apart because many fall into the trap of finding their identity in their work.

History tells us that when the Great Depression hit America in the 1930s that most of the richest men of that day committed suicide. Why is this? Because they found their identity in the money that they had earned. When their money was lost, they were lost.

IDENTITY CRISIS

Identity is everything, especially in a culture that attempts in so many different ways to tell us who we are. America has become sort of a melting pot of people who have allowed themselves to be shaped by ideologies and paradigms that wrestle against their God-given identity. If we do not know who we were created to be then we lose our identity as children of God.

In the garden of Eden, Adam and Eve walked and talked with God. They were created and placed into relationship with their Creator. The Lord breathed His Spirit into them and their entire life revolved around their relationship with God and with one another. The Lord said, *"It is not good for the man to be alone. I will make a helper suitable for him"* (Genesis 2:18). Even when the Lord made all the animals to pass by before Adam, the Bible says: *"But for Adam no suitable helper was found"* (v. 20). It was in this moment that the Lord put Adam into a deep sleep and formed Eve from his rib.

God created man for relationship. We see clearly in this passage of Genesis that He never meant for Adam to live alone in relationship with God only. There was an innate need for Adam to have a relationship with a suitable helper here on earth. The man and the woman were placed into a perfect environment that was whole and complete. They themselves found perfection in their relationship with God and with each other. This is God's perfect creation. Within His creation, we see God expressing perfect love that He has within Himself between the Father, Son and Holy Spirit. The Trinity has perfect relationship within Himself. The Father loves the Son and the Son loves His Father. The Holy Spirit glorifies both the Son and the Father; perfect love being expressed within His Presence for all eternity. God has no need within Himself because He has perfect relationship within His Triune nature.

God's ultimate heart behind His creation is His willingness to express His love to those He created. God is love, and His love is expressed through who He is, and this love is seen in all He does. He created man to be loved, and from the place of being loved we also will express His love to one another. It really is that simple! Yet, because of sin, man has lost his original identity as sons and daughters created to *be loved*.

In Genesis 3, we see this loss of identity immediately. When sin entered the hearts of Adam and Eve, the Presence of God departed. Immediately, we see God coming back to the garden looking for Adam and Eve crying out "Where are you?" The consequence of sin resulted in God rejecting man from His Presence. Amazingly, we still see the heart of the Father. In the midst of this rejection, God's response was to quickly restore the relationship that was lost as the result of Adam's sin. Those who were created to be sons and daughters of the Most High God were now slaves to the sin that they fell into. Though Adam lost his identity as the son of God, the Lord immediately prophesied of His plan for redemption (see Genesis 3:15). Though God brought judgment against sin, He also followed this judgment with His mercy. This is the heart of our God. God is a righteous judge, and in His righteousness He longs to restore relationship. It is not in His heart that those who have been cast away would remain lost outside of His Presence.

One of the many things that amazes me about the Lord is His heart to give man the opportunity to repent and confess. This is the heart of God! Religion has painted the picture of a God who is angry with the sinner, and if we don't get our lives right He is just ready and willing to throw us into hell. I will declare boldly that this is not the Father God that I see here in Genesis. I read of a Father who came looking for His children to restore the relationship that was lost. This is the God of the Bible.

The entire Old Testament is the unveiling of God's plan to restore the relationship and the identity of His children. Yes, God established a Law in Israel. Yes, God repeatedly brought judgment on Israel for their rebellion against His Law. What we must understand is that it was never in the heart of God for man to be made righteous through the works of the Law.

Therefore, no one will be declared righteous in His sight by observing the law; rather, through the law we become conscious of sin (Romans 3:20).

For God has imprisoned everyone in disobedience so He could have mercy on everyone (Romans 11:32 NLT).

What the Bible is telling us here is that our relationship with God was never to be established through our works of the Law. We will never find our identity in what we do. God created us to *be loved!*

THE BELOVED

In Genesis 3, one of the judgments pronounced to Adam was:

The ground is under a curse because of you. All your life you will struggle to scratch a living from it. It will grow thorns and thistles for you ... By the sweat of your brow will you have food to eat" (vv. 17-19 NLT).

I believe it is here, at the very beginning, as man's judgment for sin, that the "works-driven" nature took root within us. The consequence of man's sin was that we were left to be orphans, outside of the Presence and fellowship with our Father. At the core of our soul is a place, created by God, to be His resting place within us. As the consequence of sin, God left His dwelling place and cast man out of His Presence to work the ground from which he came.

This is what I have begun to call the "orphaned spirit" within fallen man. The orphaned spirit is the emptiness within us that can only be filled with the love of our Father. Humanity has spent generation after generation "working" to fill that void with everything but God. It will never work! All our attempts will only bring up thorns and thistles. Even the religions of this world, including much of Christianity at large, creates a "works-driven" relationship that demands that we earn our way into right standing with God the Father. This is man's attempt from the orphaned spirit within to earn God's love.

I am convinced that one of the hardest things for a human being to do is to sit still and "be" loved. In most of our relationships we will unknowingly give ourselves to doing all we can to earn the love of those we desire attention from. We do this because of the emptiness inside that longs to be accepted. This mindset is at the very root of the sin nature inside that can only be satisfied by being perfectly loved by God. The orphaned spirit within will always manifest in a vain attempt to earn a love that can only be received freely. Scripture tells us: "He [God] gives more grace. Therefore He says, 'God resists the proud, but gives grace to the humble'" (James

THE BELOVED BRIDE

4:6 NKJV). Grace is God's unmerited (unearned) favor and is His free gift to humanity because He is love. God's love and grace cannot be earned, it can only be received by faith in His Son Jesus. God only gives His grace to those who humble themselves before Him and receive freely from Him. It cannot be earned through work, only freely received by faith! WOW, can you not see the goodness of God?

As I've said before, it seems that one of the hardest things for a human being is to "be" loved. The prideful sin nature wants to bring something into our relationship with God that merits His love through our work. In this pride, we feel some sort of false security of being loved because we "did" right. God will resist this pride and reject these efforts, not to be mean or hurtful, but to protect us from the sin of pride. Again, pride is at the very root of the sin nature of which we have been redeemed from.

We see this displayed in Adam and Eve's first son Cain. Cain brought an offering to the Lord from the works of his own hands; his own grain and the fruit of the ground. The Lord rejected Cain's offering. Now we understand from James 4:6 that God only rejects pride. So we could say that God rejected the pride of Cain's works. So often we do the same thing unknowingly. Because of the orphaned spirit inside, we find our identity in our own works. When one finds identity in the works of their own hands then we are rejecting the grace of God that flows freely from His nature of love. *"For it is by grace that you have been saved, through faith ... not by works, so that no one can boast" (Ephesians 2:8-9).*

In the beginning God created man in His own image to be His sons and daughters. Our identity rests in who we are in Him. As sons and daughters we inherit His nature; the Divine Nature! After the sin of Adam and Eve in the garden, God was on a mission to restore the identity that we were created and placed into; sons and daughters of the Most High. God sent His only Son into the world to restore this relationship. When Jesus came, He was sent to an orphaned Israel who found their identity in the works of the Law. Christ came calling the Holy God of Israel His Abba Father. Abba is a term of endearment in the Hebrew culture. It is much like young children calling their Father "daddy." This so infuriated the religious leaders, that this became the catalyst that fueled their desire to put

Jesus to death (see John 5:18). The people of Israel lived with such emptiness from the orphaned spirit that they could never fathom approaching the Holy God as their Abba Father. They only attempted to please Him with their works. They missed the whole plan of God to restore His sons and daughters to Himself because they found their identity in the pride of their own works.

At Jesus' baptism, the Bible tells us, *"Behold, the heavens were opened to Him, and He saw the Spirit of God descending like a dove and alighting upon Him. And suddenly a voice came from heaven, saying, 'This is My Beloved Son, in whom I am well pleased'"* (Matthew 3:16-17 NKJV). Now, what we must understand is that at this time Jesus had yet to "do" anything. No sign, wonder, or miracle was recorded at this point except that Jesus, at the age of twelve, was found teaching and being taught by the priests and the scribes in the temple. The Father put the seal of sonship on Jesus before He ever did a thing. In fact, even when Jesus was driven by the Spirit into the wilderness, the devil attacked this identity: *"If you be the Son of God do this ... do this ... do this."* Satan was attacking the orphaned nature within the soul of man that finds identity through works. We must remember that Jesus was fully man and was tempted in all the same points that humanity is tempted. Jesus was, is, and always will be the Son of God by nature. When we are born again, we too enter into sonship with Jesus by the will of the Father, not by our own works but by faith in the Son of God.

We are the Beloved by faith in Jesus Christ. We were created as sons and daughters to "be loved." We are the beloved children of God. By our simple faith in the Son of God we partake in His inheritance. We are no longer orphans without a Father, but we have been adopted into sonship and can now experience the perfect love of our Abba Father in heaven. Through the shed blood of Jesus we now have royal blood flowing through our veins, which breaks all the old nature that was accustomed to pride and the fear of man. We are the Beloved, *so be loved!*

When one allows himself to "be" loved perfectly by our Abba Father, then fear is cast away (see 1 John 4:18). As sons and daughters of God we have free access into His Presence to be loved by Him. No one can ever earn His perfect love. God chooses, in His goodness, to freely love us with perfect, selfless love that will drive out all fear, doubt, shame, and every other root of darkness that separates us from His love. Sons and daughters are free to BE LOVED and therefore they love Abba Father back with the same love that we ourselves have freely received.

The Beloved sons and daughters not only love the Father but they also love one another as brothers and sisters, knit together by the perfect love that flows from our Father's Presence. This is His will from the beginning. He created sons and daughters in His image to reflect His perfect love, not only in our worship to Him but in our love for one another. As we walk in this love for one another we expel darkness in the Light of His love. This is the glory of this End Time Army!

Oh, that the Church would once again walk in our true identity as sons and daughters of God. Oh, that we would cast aside the pride of our own efforts and strivings. We have built beautiful buildings. We have well-organized denominations. We have great programs and well-orchestrated Sunday morning services; *but we are absent of the perfect love of Abba Father being lived out through Beloved Sons and Daughters! LORD, HELP US IN THIS HOUR!*

THE BRIDE

The Father has rescued us by sending His only Son to reconcile us back to Himself in love. We are now His children because of the blood of His Son Jesus. Yet there is one important key to sending His Son that I believe is the final piece of this puzzle for the End Time Army that is on the front lines in this hour.

In the book of Revelation, John the beloved tells of a vision that he had of a city coming down from heaven like *"a bride beautifully dressed for her husband" (Revelation 21:2).* He then tells us that one of the angels that holds one of the seven last plagues came to him and said *"Come, and I will show you the bride, the wife of the Lamb" (v. 9).* This angel then takes him through this "city" and shows him all the beauty and the decor of this "bride."

So who is this "bride"? Is it a physical city? I have heard some teach of the New Jerusalem as a physical city and that might be partially correct. Yet I will answer boldly who this bride is! *It is you and I. We are the bride of the Lamb of God, Jesus Christ!* God the Father sent His only Son to rescue and redeem us back unto the Father. Yet, as awesome as this is, He also loves His Son and He sent Him to prepare a bride for Himself. We are His bride!

Our identity is found in us as sons and daughters of our Abba Father, but equally so, we are the bride of His Son Jesus. I believe our identity as the bride is absolutely key in this last hour. Why? In Revelation 22 John records the last written words of Jesus saying: *"Behold, I am coming soon! My reward is with Me ... I, Jesus, have sent My angel to give you this testimony for the churches" (Revelation 22:12,16 NIV).* In the same breath that Jesus is speaking, John hears and records, *"The Spirit and the bride say, 'Come'" (v. 17).* Notice it is the cry of the Spirit and the bride that are coupled together in the last hour before Jesus comes. It is not the Spirit and the warriors. It is not the Spirit and the intercessors. Nor is it the Spirit and the five-fold ministers. In the last hour there is a consummation of the groanings of the Holy Spirit, coupled together with the worship and adoration of a lovesick bride, that will usher in His second coming.

The fuel for the End Time Army will be burning love! In the Song of Solomon, the bride cries out to her bridegroom,

> *Place me like a seal over your heart, like a seal on your arm; for love is as strong as death, its jealousy unyielding as the grave. It burns like blazing fire, like a mighty flame. Many waters cannot quench love* (8:6-7).

The Song of Solomon is one of the greatest books in the Bible that reveals the intimate love affair between a husband and his wife. When read with prophetic eyes, the Song of Solomon is a revelation into the love of the Bridegroom Jesus and His bride, the church! When all is said and done, the church is being prepared as the bride of Christ and we will sit and enjoy the marriage supper of the Lamb when we meet our Lord.

THE BELOVED BRIDE

There is a bride that is preparing herself in this hour that is longing to be with her Bridegroom. Man and woman alike, *we are His bride!* How is she preparing herself? In the place of worship! Worship, in its purest form, is being in love. The bride's place of preparation is the altar of worship where she is lifting her love up before her Bridegroom and having intimacy in the secret place with Him.

The Lord is releasing His perfect love onto the Earth in this hour like never before. As the church, who is His bride, receives this perfect love, we will love Him back with the same love that He loves us with. This is worship: loving God with His perfect love and pouring our burning love back on Him. The greatest picture of this kind of intimate love is the marriage between a husband and a wife.

God chose to reveal the bride of Christ in the last book of Holy Scripture. Yet, when we also understand that Jesus is the First and the Last, the Beginning and the End, the Alpha and the Omega, then we can also see the end at the beginning. Let me explain. In the garden of Eden, God created Adam. When God saw that it was was not good for him to be alone, he brought forth his bride, Eve, from Adam's side. Paul reveals this mystery in his letter to the Ephesians while teaching husbands and wives how to live together in love. He likens marriages in the natural to our relationship with Christ and finishes by taking us back to Genesis:

> For this reason a man will leave his father and mother and be united to his wife, and the two will become one flesh. This is a profound mystery— but I am talking about Christ and the church (Ephesians 5:31, 32).

We see the plan of God all the way back in the beginning. Adam is a type of the Son of God and Eve is a type of the bride. Paul reveals this to us in Romans 5 and again in 1 Corinthians 15. We see in the beginning the plan of God joining His Son with the bride that was brought forth from His side. Jesus left His Father's house in heaven and will be joined with His bride in the end and the two will become one flesh. Oh, how rich is the Word of God!

This End Time Army is going to come back into our identity as sons and daughters and the bride of Christ. A two-fold purpose within our existence—our identity in the eyes of our Father and our identity in the eyes of the Son. It's not about how we see ourselves, but it is about how HE sees us!

When we walk in the love of God then we will reflect this same love into the darkness of this hour. The bride will walk in such flaming love for the Bridegroom that even death itself will not hold them back from contending in the place of worship and prayer. Paul tells us in Romans 8 that all creation is groaning for the manifestation of the sons and daughters of God. He also says that the Spirit itself is making intercession for us with groanings that cannot be uttered. In the midst of all the groaning and travailing, the bride of Christ is making herself ready in the secret place and is joining with all creation and the Holy Spirit in the yearnings of heaven. She will be burning with such passionate love for her Bridegroom King that she will not be able to live without Him any longer.

I believe that we are living in the last hour as the groanings of all creation, the groanings of the Holy Spirit, and the yearning of a lovesick bride are rising up before the throne room in heaven as a sweet incense before our God and the Lamb! I am convinced that the hour is at hand that a generation is being marked with burning, lovesick devotion that is creating a sound of worship that will finally compel the Bridegroom to come and take His bride for Himself. She has made herself ready at the altar of worship and adoration where she is pouring out her love before the courts of heaven. Through this love, a voice is petitioning the Son of God crying, "Come Lord! Come Lord! You are the Lover of my soul and I can't live without you any longer!" The heart of Jesus is being so moved by this perfect love towards Him that He cannot help but respond by coming and taking His rightful place as King of all with His bride at His side.

OUR TRUE IDENTITY

I have said this many times before, but it's worth saying again: *Worship is not what we do, it is who we are!* We were created as worshipers to be loved and to reciprocate that love back towards the throne of God. Our identity was established by God as sons and daughters of God the Father. The Father then sent His Son to prepare a bride for Himself.

As sons and daughters and as His bride we have been restored to our original place with God in His garden, the paradise of God. In this place we tend His Presence by worshipping and serving the Lord with His perfect, selfless love that He pours into us. We have the honor of giving back to God the same love that He has given to us. As we fan the flames of love for God in the place of worship, His love will freely flow through us towards others. This is the purpose behind God creating man in His image; to reflect His love back towards Him as both Father and Bridegroom. When we walk in right relationship with God, then we will also reflect this same love towards one another. No matter how dark the situation, we will reflect the light of His love into the darkness and it will flee before us.

Our true identity is found in Him. It is not found in our works, but only as we fall in love with Him will He mark us with true identity and purpose. Our Abba Father is perfect in all His ways. His Son Jesus loves His bride with the same love that the Triune God has within Himself. This is the fuel for true worship and it is the key that will unlock the everlasting doors for the King of Glory to come in the last hour. This is the true identity of the End Time Army of Worshipers. Let us walk in our true identity and make ready the world for the second coming of the Bridegroom King Jesus!

Chapter 12

WARRING FROM HIS PRESENCE

As you conclude this book, I must ask: "Are you ready to enlist in this army, and are you ready to jump onto the front lines of this age-old battle?"

My one prayer for all who read this book is that they will see that God is smashing the old paradigms of how this war is fought. God is raising up an army that no longer has to pound their fists into the ground, screaming at the devil to leave their cities. He is raising up an army that does not war according to the ways of this present world. *"For though we live in the world, we do not wage war as the world does. The weapons we fight with are not weapons of the world. On the contrary, they have divine power to demolish strongholds" (2 Corinthians 10:3-4 NIV).* We now war from the place of being in love!

I can remember when this revelation hit home for me. It was during a very stressful season during youth pastoring. It seemed like the weight of the spiritual warfare against us was more than my wife and I could bear. We were dealing with the sins of someone who was very close to our hearts and it was affecting so many others around us. It seemed like the devil was having his way in this matter and he was laughing in our faces.

In my zeal for the Lord I began to take up the Sword of the Spirit and fight back. My sermons began to be harder and harder against sin and became consistently focused on evil and the devil. Even in my prayer time,

I was constantly feeling the pressure to bind and rebuke the devil. Often times if I didn't pray until I was sweating and my jaw hurt from praying so hard in tongues, I did not believe that my prayers touched heaven. I became more weighed down by circumstances and more angry at sin and the devil.

This season all culminated one weekend as my wife and I were blessed to get away to the mountains of Chico, California, and the YWAM base up there. This base is an absolutely beautiful, secluded spot in the Sierra Nevada Mountains. The moment we arrived, it seemed that the weights of life that we were carrying just slid off of our backs. We unpacked and immediately went for a hike and found this solitary place overlooking the valley. From here we went to separate spots to fellowship alone with God.

It was here that God spoke to me in a place of restful quietness and changed my life. He said, *"It is in this place of rest that you must learn to fight in this war. I have already won this battle and you must rest in this place where it is finished. The devil is trying to pull you out of My resting place into his arena of hatred and anger against sin and evil. You must fight from My love and peace."* This word from heaven shifted something inside of me forever. I immediately grasped what God was saying to me and healing took place right there and has continued to this day.

This End Time Worship Army is called to fight from the place of love and passion for the Presence of God. We will never endure the coming hour if we allow the enemy to pull us out of loving His Presence into a carnal striving and contending to win a war that has already been won. The heart of David prophesied that he would not give sleep to his eyes until he found this place for God—a resting place for the Lord (see Psalm 132). This word has now become the message of my life: to stir a generation into joining this End Time Worship Army.

Our warfare must come from the place of rest in His Presence. This is the army that God is raising up in this hour. This army will sit at the table that the Lord has prepared for them, even in the presence of their enemies (see Psalm 23). They have learned to enjoy His Presence even in the face of great opposition. This voluntary act of humility and love breaks the back of the enemy.

The Lord Himself spoke, *"The ruler of this world is coming, and he has nothing in Me" (John 14:30).* The Lord was making a faith-filled statement that the enemy was not going to find anything within Him that could pull Him out of His rest in His Father. Jesus had all authority to call legions of angels to fight against hell in His hour of need. Yet it was His voluntary humility to obey His Father even to His death on the cross that broke the power of darkness over all humanity.

So it is now with us! Though we may have all authority to bind, rebuke, cut and tear the demonic realm, it will be our voluntary submission to fall upon the altars of worship, in love with the Presence of God, that will push principalities and powers out of our cities and regions.

Are you ready to jump on the front lines now? Will you play your part in this End Time Worship Army? We all need one another in our places of radically loving God and radically loving one another. It is this violent love that will prophecy to the world that we are disciples of the Bridegroom Jesus Christ. Let us join together and prepare our cities and nations for the coming of the Bridegroom King until, *"The kingdoms of the world have become the kingdoms of our God and His Christ" (Revelation 11:15).*

ENDNOTES

Chapter 1:

1. Spiros Zodhiates, *Hebrew/Greek Keyword Study Bible, New International Version,* (AMG International 1996), p.1514.
2. W.E Vines, *Vine's Concise Dictionary of the Bible*, (Thomas Nelson, Inc. 2005) p. 225.

Chapter 3:

1. James Strong, *Strong's Exhaustive Concordance*, (Thomas Nelson Publishing 1990) p. 106.

Chapter 5:

1. Spiros Zodhiates, *op.cit.,* p. 1662.

Chapter 6:

1. Spiros Zodhiates, *op.cit.,* p. 1601.
2. Spiros Zodhiates, *op.cit.,* p. 1550.

Chapter 7:

1. Spiros Zodhiates, *op.cit.,* p. 1650.

Chapter 9:

1. Spiros Zodhiates, *op.cit.,* p. 1562.

Chapter 10:

1. James Strong, *op.cit.,* p. 121.

Printed in Great Britain
by Amazon.co.uk, Ltd.,
Marston Gate.